ROSSIAN ETHICS

ROSSIAN ETHICS

*W.D. Ross and Contemporary
Moral Theory*

DAVID PHILLIPS

OXFORD
UNIVERSITY PRESS

Oxford University Press is a department of the University of Oxford. It furthers
the University's objective of excellence in research, scholarship, and education
by publishing worldwide. Oxford is a registered trade mark of Oxford University
Press in the UK and certain other countries.

Published in the United States of America by Oxford University Press
198 Madison Avenue, New York, NY 10016, United States of America.

Library of Congress Cataloging-in-Publication Data
Names: Phillips, David (David K.), author.
Title: Rossian ethics : W.D. Ross and contemporary
moral theory / David Phillips.
Description: New York : Oxford University Press, 2019. |
Includes bibliographical references and index.
Identifiers: LCCN 2018051609 (print) | LCCN 2019015034 (ebook) |
ISBN 9780190602192 (updf) | ISBN 9780190602208 (online content) |
ISBN 9780190054656 (epub) | ISBN 9780190602185 (cloth : alk. paper)
Subjects: LCSH: Ross, W. D. (William David), 1877–1971.
Classification: LCC BJ654.R673 (ebook) |
LCC BJ654.R673 P45 2019 (print) | DDC 171/.2—dc23
LC record available at https://lccn.loc.gov/2018051609

9 8 7 6 5 4 3 2 1

Printed by Sheridan Books, Inc., United States of America

To Susan

CONTENTS

ACKNOWLEDGMENTS

I have been extremely fortunate in the help I have received with this project. Peter Ohlin and his colleagues at Oxford University Press have been characteristically encouraging and professional throughout; and I am particularly grateful for their flexibility as work on the final draft was rescheduled by Hurricane Harvey. The two referees, David McNaughton and Anthony Skelton, provided invaluable feedback which shaped the book in fundamental ways. Two of my colleagues, Justin Coates and Luis Oliveira, read the entire manuscript at different stages and helped me tremendously with many suggestions for improvements and much guidance on contemporary literature. Jonathan Dancy, Jamie Dreier, and George Sher gave acute and helpful comments on drafts of individual chapters and sections. And Ed Sherline and an audience at the Rocky Mountain Ethics Congress in 2015 provided very enlightening feedback on a version of chapter 3.

None of them, of course, is responsible for the book's no doubt numerous remaining flaws.

INTRODUCTION

I HAVE TWO CONNECTED AIMS in this book. The first is to interpret and critically evaluate W. D. Ross's moral philosophy. The second is to develop a distinctive normative view. The two aims are connected because the normative view can be developed, as I will develop it, as an interpretation of Ross. But they are also separable: it would be perfectly possible to find the normative view attractive in itself but misconceived as a reading of Ross.

Let me say a little more about each aim. As to the first: Ross's most important works in moral philosophy, *The Right and the Good* and *Foundations of Ethics*, contain significant discussions both of metaethics and of moral theory.[1] My main focus will be Ross's moral theory, which I think more important and more distinctive than his metaethics. His metaethics is largely a sophisticated development of views articulated before him by Sidgwick, Moore, and others;[2] and insofar as his views in moral epistemology are distinctive, I shall argue that they are mistaken. His moral theory is something new, different both from Sidgwick's hedonistic utilitarianism and from Moore's ideal utilitarianism; and I shall argue that what is new in it is importantly right.

As to the second aim: many opponents of consequentialism, from Kant to Anscombe to the present, regard it with hostility and contempt. But a quite different attitude is possible: the attitude that consequentialism is partly true but not the whole truth; that the reason to promote the good is very important but not our only reason. I think Ross is the best source in the historical tradition for this kind of respectful rejection of consequentialism. And I think a distinctive alternative to traditional consequentialism can be found in and developed from his work, a view that is worth serious consideration in contemporary moral theory.[3]

It will be helpful to have a name for the distinctive normative view I will find in Ross. The name I will use is "classical deontology."[4] Classical deontology is a view about the nature of the most fundamental normative truths. According to classical deontology the most fundamental normative principles are principles of prima facie duty,[5] principles which specify general kinds of reasons. Utilitarians are right to think that reasons always derive from goods; and ideal utilitarians are right, contra hedonistic utilitarians, to think that there are a small number of distinct kinds of intrinsic goods. But consequentialists are wrong to think that all reasons have the same weight for all agents. Instead, there are a small number of distinct kinds of agent-relative intensifiers: features that increase the weight of certain reasons for certain agents. The key problem with consequentialism is that it misses "the highly personal character of duty," the special agent-relative weight of promises, gratitude, and reparation.

I don't think the kind of project I am undertaking here is especially novel, either in the history of philosophy in general or in the history of ethics in particular. At the start of *The Bounds of Sense*, P. F. Strawson writes,[6]

I have tried to present a clear, uncluttered and unified interpretation, at least strongly supported by the text as it stands,
of the system of thought which the *Critique* contains; I have
tried to show how certain great parts of the structure can be
held apart from each other, while showing also how, within the
system itself, they are conceived of as related; I have tried to
give decisive reasons for rejecting some parts altogether; and
I have tried to indicate, though no more than indicate, how the
arguments and conclusions of other parts might be so modified or reconstructed as to be made more acceptable.

In a similar vein, at the start of *Hobbesian Moral and Political
Theory*, Gregory Kavka writes,[7]

> Though he has been more than three hundred years in the
> grave, Thomas Hobbes still has much to teach us. His works
> identify enduring problems of social and political life and
> suggest some promising solutions for them. Yet, at the same
> time, they contain important errors. . . . To learn the most
> from Hobbes, we must correct or avoid these errors, while
> preserving and building upon the fundamentally sound philo-
> sophical structure they infest.
>
> With that aim in mind, this book offers an explicitly re-
> visionist interpretation of Hobbes's moral and political
> philosophy. . . . The ultimate goal of this process is to ex-
> plicate and defend a plausible system of moral and political
> hypotheses suggested and inspired by Hobbes. Throughout,
> an attempt is made to indicate clearly which of the views
> discussed are Hobbes's and which are proposed alterations
> or improvements of his position. Because the modifications
> offered are not trivial, it would be misleading to describe the
> theory propounded here as that of Hobbes. Even where it
> departs from his position, however, the theory resembles his
> in critical respects.

Strawson's and Kavka's projects have the same character as mine. But, focused as they are on Kant and Hobbes respectively, they are models, not competitors. One philosophical project, however, is, I take it, both a model for and a competitor with mine: Robert Audi's defense of "value-based intuitionism."[8] Value-based intuitionism is a blend of Rossian and Kantian ideas. Audi could (and I take it he does) argue that the best philosophical interpretation of Ross is that Ross is a value-based intuitionist. This is not supposed to be true by definition. And it is not supposed to be true because everything Ross says fits value-based intuitionism—some of what Ross explicitly says conflicts with value-based intuitionism. It is supposed to be true rather because, Audi thinks, the best way to make philosophical sense of Ross—to attribute to Ross a view that matches much of what he says and is independently philosophically plausible—is to understand him as a value-based intuitionist. I will be arguing (contra Audi) that the best philosophical interpretation of Ross is as a classical deontologist. Like Audi, I will not take my interpretive claim to be true by definition. Rather, I will be arguing that the best way to make philosophical sense of Ross—to attribute to him a view that matches much of what he says and is independently philosophically plausible—is to understand him as a classical deontologist.

Any philosophical project like Audi's, Kavka's, Strawson's, or mine involves two potentially conflicting prima facie philosophical duties—to interpret the texts faithfully, and to develop the most plausible philosophical view. A Rossian might well deny that there is any helpful general rule about how to balance these prima facie philosophical duties against one another.

Ross's distinctive philosophical views did not arise in a vacuum. They developed by acquaintance with and reflection on the ideas of earlier central figures in the British intuitionist tradition, which stretches, as Thomas Hurka has persuasively argued, from Sidgwick to Ewing.[9] Prichard and Moore were particularly important to him. They are the two influences he mentions by name in the preface to *The Right and the Good*. Of Prichard he says:

> My main obligation is to Professor H. A. Prichard. I believe I owe the main lines of the view expressed in my first two chapters to his article "Does Moral Philosophy rest on a Mistake?"[10] (RG v)

He goes on to say:

> I also wish to say how much I owe to Professor G. E. Moore's writings. A glance at the index will show how much I have referred to him. (RG v)

And indeed there are more references to Moore in the index of *The Right and the Good* than there are to any other philosopher.

There is also a particularly close relationship between Ross's work and some of C. D. Broad's. In *Five Types of Ethical Theory*,[11] published in the very same year as *The Right and the Good*, Broad arrived independently at views strikingly like Ross's. In the later *Foundations of Ethics* (1939), Ross noted this similarity:

> In the main, Professor Broad's view is just that which I wish to advocate, viz. that among the features of a situation that tend to make an act right there are some which are independent of

the tendency of the act to bring about a maximum of good. To say this is to hold an intuitionistic view of one kind. (F 82)

And Broad responded enthusiastically to Ross's work, observing in his review of the *Foundations*,

> The Provost of Oriel's book, *The Right and the Good*, published in 1930, was much the most important contribution to ethical theory made in England for a generation,

and concluding,

> I hope that generations of undergraduates, in the intervals between making the world safer and safer for democracy, will come to know and appreciate this book under the affectionate and accurate nickname of *"The Righter and the Better."*[12]

My interpretive target here is Ross, not Prichard or Broad (or Moore). But I will draw freely on Prichard and Broad in developing my interpretation of Ross.

I hope, of course, to make a convincing case for interpreting Ross as a classical deontologist. But I hope that those who are not convinced will still find the discussion of Ross illuminating: that they will think the questions I raise about how to place Ross within contemporary moral theory and how to understand the core of his opposition to consequentialism are important questions, even if they think I give them the wrong answers.

This study will have four further substantive chapters. In the first three I consider in turn the three central elements of Ross's normative view: the concept of prima facie duty, the moderate pluralism about the right, and the moderate

pluralism about the good. I begin in chapter 2 with the concept of prima facie duty. Ross introduces it to address the
objection that deontology is rendered incoherent by conflicts
of duty. I raise two central interpretive issues, about the characterization of prima facie duty and the structure of an ethics
based upon it, and about whether Ross's central normative
claims are best understood as claims about morality or as
claims about normative reasons. And I argue that Ross was
wrong in the *Foundations* to follow Prichard in prioritizing
subjective rather than objective rightness. In chapter 3 I turn
to Ross's moderate pluralism about the right. I focus on his
diagnosis of ideal utilitarianism as missing "the highly personal character of duty." I argue that almost everything on
his list of underived prima facie duties consists either (a) of
duties to promote the good or (b) of what he calls "special
obligations": reasons to keep promises, repay wrongs, and
manifest gratitude. I argue that these special obligations are
(what I call) "agent-relative intensifiers" of reasons to promote goods. I argue that if we understand deontological
reasons as consisting only of (b) we can avoid problems with
standard deontology. I argue, following Sidgwick, that there
are other agent-relative intensifiers Ross himself does not recognize. And I argue that the normative theory that all reason-
giving features are either goods or agent-relative intensifiers
of reasons to promote goods is distinctive and attractive.
In chapter 4 I turn to Ross's moderate pluralism about the
good. I begin with aspects of his view with which I am sympathetic: his provisional list of intrinsic goods, virtue, knowledge, pleasure, and the proportioning of pleasure to virtue;
and his appeal to intuitions about the relative goodness of
quite abstractly described possible worlds to defend the
list. But I argue against his position on the relative value of

different goods. In different ways in *The Right and the Good* and the *Foundations* Ross is a radical antihedonist, arguing that virtue is in some way systematically more valuable than pleasure. I reject both his (excessively negative) treatment of pleasure and his (excessively positive) treatment of virtue. Finally I ask whether Ross's list of intrinsic goods is exhaustive. I argue that it is at the least a very plausible core list and that Ross's explanation of its unity is helpful in assessing possible additions. In chapter 5 I consider the metaethical and epistemological framework within which Ross develops his normative views. I argue that the metaethical framework is plausible and defensible on the whole, though problematic in various important details. But I argue that Ross's distinctive views in moral epistemology should be rejected.

My interpretation of Ross is the product of a range of specific judgments of interpretive and philosophical plausibility. But it is also, as I indicated above, shaped by a guiding idea: that Ross develops a version of deontology that is close to consequentialism and a product of important modifications to consequentialism. One way to approach that guiding idea is historical. Ross is the clearest and most articulate opponent of consequentialism and utilitarianism in the Sidgwick-to-Ewing school; so of course we should look to him for reasons to reject consequentialism. But he doesn't show the hostility to consequentialism characteristic of Kantians and some other more recent deontologists. What we should look for in reading him is a theory that is consequentialism *plus*: that allows that consequentialists are right that there are goods, and that we have a duty to promote them, and that this is one crucial truth about the normative; but denies that it is the whole truth. If (as the title of a paper by Hurka has it) Audi offers "a marriage of Ross and Kant," what I suggest by contrast might be characterized as "a marriage of Ross and Sidgwick."[13] For not only do I emphasize in general the ways in which Ross is a friendly rather than a hostile critic of consequentialism; the ways in which I suggest a revisionary reading of Ross all bring him closer to Sidgwick.

NOTES

1. W. D. Ross, *The Right and the Good* (Oxford: Clarendon Press, 1930). I will refer to it as "RG"; page references will be placed in the text. W. D. Ross, *Foundations of Ethics* (Oxford: Clarendon Press, 1939). I will refer to it as "F"; page references will be placed in the text. While at least chapter 2 of *The Right and the Good* has long been quite widely read, the *Foundations* was till recently much less studied. I think both are essential for understanding and evaluating Ross's contribution to moral philosophy. Ross also published other work in moral philosophy, in chronological order: a chapter (chapter 7) in *Aristotle* (London: Methuen, 1923); four articles leading up to *The Right and the Good*: "The Basis of Objective Judgments in Ethics," *International Journal of Ethics* 37.2 (1927): 113–27; "Is There a Moral End?," *Proceedings of the Aristotelian Society: Supplementary Volumes* 8 (1928): 91–98; "The Nature of Morally Good Action," *Proceedings of the Aristotelian Society*, new series, 29 (1928–29): 251–74; "The Ethics of Punishment," *Journal of Philosophical Studies* 4.14 (April 1929): 205–11; one article between *The Right and the Good* and the *Foundations*: "The Coherence Theory of Goodness," *Proceedings of the Aristotelian Society: Supplementary Volumes* 10 (1931): 61–70; and the later *Kant's Ethical Theory* (Oxford: Clarendon Press, 1954). In my judgment none of this other work is nearly as important as *The Right and the Good* and the *Foundations*.
2. Henry Sidgwick, *The Methods of Ethics*, 7th ed. (London: Macmillan, 1907). I will refer to it as "ME"; further page references will be placed in the text. G. E. Moore, *Principia Ethica* (Cambridge: Cambridge University Press, 1903). I will

refer to it as *"Principia"*; further page references will be placed in the text.

3. Some remarks on terminology are called for. By "consequentialism" I will mean what might also be called "traditional consequentialism": the agent-neutral thesis endorsed both by hedonistic utilitarians and by ideal utilitarians like Moore according to which, as Ross puts it (RG 17), "what produces the maximum good is right." Ross himself has no name for this thesis. In *Five Types of Ethical Theory* (London: Kegan Paul, 1930), Broad does introduce a name. He calls theories according to which "the rightness or wrongness of an action is always determined by its tendency to produce certain consequences which are intrinsically good or bad" *teleological* theories (206–7). He contrasts them with *deontological* theories. In so doing, he introduces the term "deontology" in its now standard philosophical sense: "I would first divide ethical theories into two classes, which I will call respectively *deontological* and *teleological*. Deontological theories hold that there are ethical propositions of the form: 'Such and such a kind of action would always be right (or wrong) in such and such circumstances, no matter what the consequences might be'" (206). While "deontological" and "deontology" stuck, "teleological" and "teleology" were replaced by "consequentialist" and "consequentialism," terms introduced by Anscombe in "Modern Moral Philosophy," *Philosophy* 33 (1958): 1–19. For discussions of the history of the term "deontology," see Robert Louden, "Towards a Genealogy of 'Deontology,'" *Journal of the History of Philosophy* 34.4 (1996): 571–92 and Jens Timmerman, "What's Wrong with 'Deontology'?," *Proceedings of the Aristotelian Society* 115 (2015): 75–92.

In recent years a sophisticated literature has developed focused on the possibility of "consequentializing" supposedly nonconsequentialist moral and normative theories. Important work in this literature includes Jamie Dreier, "In Defense of Consequentializing," in Mark Timmons, ed., *Oxford Studies in Normative Ethics*, vol. 1 (New York: Oxford University Press, 2011), 97–119; Douglas Portmore, "Consequentializing Moral Theories," *Pacific Philosophical Quarterly* 88 (2007): 39–73, and *Commonsense Consequentialism* (New York: Oxford University Press, 2011) (especially chapter 4); and Campbell Brown, "Consequentialize This!," *Ethics* 121.4 (2011): 739–71. A key claim in this literature is what Portmore calls "the deontic equivalence thesis" and Dreier "the extensional equivalence thesis": that all plausible moral theories can be represented as forms of consequentialism. Unless I specify otherwise, I will not be using "consequentialism" and cognate terms in this broad way. I say more about consequentializing and its implications for the project of this book in chapter 3.

4. My justification for "classical" is that the form of deontology in question was suggested by the philosopher—Broad—who introduced the term "deontology" in its now standard philosophical sense. I also considered "Rossian deontology," but thought it too likely to suggest that the question how to interpret Ross was not substantive. As I say in what follows, I do intend it to be a substantive question whether Ross is best interpreted as a classical deontologist or as (for example) a value-based intuitionist.

5. Unlike Ross, who standardly italicizes "prima facie," I will not do so to avoid cluttering the text with italics.

6. P. F. Strawson, *The Bounds of Sense* (London: Methuen, 1966), 11.

7. Gregory Kavka, *Hobbesian Moral and Political Theory* (Princeton: Princeton University Press, 1986), 3.

8. See in particular Robert Audi, *The Good in the Right* (Princeton: Princeton University Press, 2004).

9. For these ideas, see in particular Thomas Hurka, "Moore in the Middle," *Ethics* 113 (2003): 599–628; "Introduction" and "Common Themes from Sidgwick to Ewing," in Thomas Hurka, ed., *Underivative Duty* (Oxford: Oxford University Press, 2011); and, for the fullest presentation, Thomas Hurka, *British Ethical Theorists from Sidgwick to Ewing* (Oxford: Oxford University Press, 2014). Hurka initially presented his view as a corrective to the idea that Moore's work represented a "clean break" from earlier ethical theorizing. (Interestingly, though of course she is much less of a fan than Hurka, Anscombe also identifies something like a Sidgwick-to-Ewing school in

"Modern Moral Philosophy." The difference between her and Hurka is that she includes the postwar "Oxford Moralists," including Hare and Nowell-Smith, as well as the prewar "Oxford Objectivists" like Ross.) For a brief expression of skepticism about whether the philosophers Hurka includes constitute a school see Bart Schultz's review of *Underivative Duty, British Journal for the History of Philosophy* 20.6 (2012): 1223–26. One might object, as Schultz there does, that Hurka's conception of the dimensions of the school is too expansive. One might alternatively object that his conception is too restrictive, and that earlier important rational intuitionists like Clarke and Price should be included too. Ross refers to Clarke and Price only once in RG and the *Foundations*: in a note on page 54 of the *Foundations* about defining rightness in terms of fitness or suitability. The eighteenth-century figure he cites more and seems more deeply influenced by is Butler. He quotes at length from the *Dissertation on the Nature of Virtue* on pages 78–79 of the *Foundations* in arguing against utilitarianism; and (as I discuss in chapter 4), the differences between his treatment of moral goodness in *The Right and the Good* and the *Foundations* are to a large extent the product of complicating the psychological picture by incorporating Butler's distinction between general and particular desires.

10. H. A. Prichard, "Does Moral Philosophy Rest on a Mistake?" *Mind* 21 (January 1912): 21–37.
11. C. D. Broad, *Five Types of Ethical Theory* (London: Routledge and Kegan Paul, 1930). I will refer to it as *Five Types*; further page references will be placed in the text.
12. C. D. Broad, "Critical Notice of W. D. Ross, *Foundations of Ethics* (Oxford, 1939)," *Mind*, new series, 49 (April 1940): 239.
13. Thomas Hurka, "Audi's Marriage of Ross and Kant," chapter 6 in Mark Timmons, John Greco, and Al. Mele, eds., *Rationality and the Good* (Oxford: Oxford University Press, 2007).

2

WHAT ARE PRIMA

FACIE DUTIES?

ROSS'S MOST IMPORTANT CONCEPTUAL INNOVATION is the idea of prima facie duty. He introduces the term on page 19 of *The Right and the Good*:

> I suggest "*prima facie* duty" or "conditional duty" as a brief way of referring to the characteristic (quite distinct from that of being a duty proper) which an act has, in virtue of being of a certain kind (e.g. the keeping of a promise), of being an act that would be a duty proper if it were not at the same time of another kind which is morally significant. Whether an act is a duty proper or actual duty depends on *all* the morally signifi-cant kinds it is an instance of. (RG 19–20)

Later he characterizes prima facie duties as "tendencies," compares them to physical forces, and distinguishes prima facie duties as "parti-resultant attributes" from duties which are "toti-resultant attributes":

> We have to distinguish from the characteristic of being our duty that of tending to be our duty. Any act that we do contains various elements in virtue of which it falls under various categories. In virtue of being the breaking of a promise, for

instance, it tends to be wrong; in virtue of being an instance of relieving distress it tends to be right. Tendency to be one's duty may be called a parti-resultant attribute, i.e. one which belongs to an act in virtue of some one component in its nature. *Being* one's duty is a toti-resultant attribute, one which belongs to an act in virtue of its whole nature and of nothing less than this. . . . Another instance of the same distinction may be found in the operation of natural laws. *Qua* subject to the force of gravitation towards some other body, each body tends to move in a particular direction with a particular velocity; but its actual movement depends on *all* the forces to which it is subject. (RG 28–29)

The main argument for introducing the concept of prima facie duty is that it allows the deontologist to avoid familiar objections to simple absolutist deontology. The most standard such objection is that duties may conflict, and that in the face of conflicts of duty deontology is rendered incoherent. Ross explains very clearly in the *Foundations* how the concept of prima facie duty helps the deontologist solve or dissolve this problem:

It is the overlooking of the distinction . . . between actual obligatoriness and the tendency to be obligatory, that leads to the apparent problem of conflict of duties, and it is by drawing the distinction that we solve the problem, or rather show it to be non-existent. For while an act may well be *prima facie* obligatory in respect of one character and *prima facie* forbidden in virtue of another, it becomes obligatory or forbidden only in virtue of the totality of its ethically relevant characteristics. We are perfectly familiar with this way of thinking when we are face to face with actual problems of conduct, but in theories of ethics responsibilities have often been overstated as being absolute obligations admitting of no exception, and the

WHAT ARE PRIMA FACIE DUTIES? | 15

unreal problem of conflict of duties has thus been supposed to exist. (F 86)

A related but more historical point concerns Sidgwick's critique of absolutist deontology (what he calls "dogmatic intuitionism") in the *Methods*. Like many earlier readers, though not so many more recent ones,[1] Broad in *Five Types of Ethical Theory* finds Sidgwick's critique convincing:

> I think that anyone who reads the relevant chapters in Sidgwick will agree that the extreme form of Intuitionism which he ascribes to common-sense cannot be maintained. And he is no doubt right that common-sense wants to hold something like this, and retreats from it only at the point of the bayonet. (*Five Types*, 217)

But rather than agree with Sidgwick that the only alternative is a mainly teleological view, it is at this point that Broad, working (so far as I know and can tell) quite independently of Ross, sketches an alternative "form of Intuitionism which is not open to Sidgwick's objections," featuring, inter alia, a version of the concept of prima facie duty developed in terms of fittingness, which (as we will see) Ross goes on largely to endorse in the *Foundations*. Broad suggests that actions have two quite different kinds of ethical features,

> fittingness or unfittingness . . . and . . . utility or disutility. . . . Fittingness or unfittingness is a direct ethical relation between an action or emotion and the total course of events in which it takes place. . . . It is quite easy to give examples. . . . I may be an elector to an office, and one of the candidates may have done me a service. To prefer him to a better qualified candidate

would fit one aspect of the situation, since it would be re-
warding a benefactor. (*Five Types*, 219)

And he remarks that

> It seems quite clear that the Intuitionist will have to moderate
> his claims very greatly. He will be confined to statements about
> *tendencies* to be right and *tendencies* to be wrong. He can say
> that a lie has a very strong tendency to be wrong, and that it will
> be wrong unless telling the truth would have very great disutility
> or unless the situation be of a certain very special kind in which
> it is a matter of honour to shield a third person. (*Five Types*, 222)

Ewing observed that the concept of prima facie duty
was "one of the most important discoveries of the century in
moral philosophy."[2] But its importance does not mean that
the concept is unproblematic or that the character of the conceptual scheme in which it plays a key role is immediately
clear. Ross himself was dissatisfied with the name "prima
facie duty." Various later theorists went further in criticizing
his characterizations of it. And while Ross did not use the
concept of a normative reason, its ubiquity in contemporary
philosophical ethics means that any reconstruction of Ross
must consider whether prima facie duties are just normative
reasons, or, if not, how to understand the relationship between prima facie duties and normative reasons.

My aim in this chapter is to explore these issues. I will
begin by asking about the coherence and adequacy of Ross's
treatment of the concept of prima facie duty in its original
philosophical context. I will then ask what to make of his
views once we introduce the contemporary concept of a
normative reason. And I will turn finally to the questions
whether Ross is or ought to be a scalar deontologist, and

whether he was right in the *Foundations* to follow Prichard in prioritizing subjective over objective rightness.

1. PRIMA FACIE DUTY: CHARACTERIZATION

Concerns about the characterization and definition of prima facie duty begin with Ross himself. Immediately after introducing the term he apologizes:

> The phrase, *"prima facie* duty" must be apologized for, since (1) it suggests that what we are speaking of is a kind of duty, whereas it is in fact not a duty, but something related in a special way to duty. Strictly speaking, we want not a phrase in which duty is qualified by an adjective, but a separate noun. (2) *"Prima"* facie suggests that one is speaking only of an appearance which a moral situation presents at first sight, and which may turn out to be illusory; whereas what I am speaking of is an objective fact involved in the nature of the situation, or more strictly in an element of its nature. (RG 20)

He considers, in *The Right and the Good* and in the *Foundations*, Prichard's alternative suggestion, "claim," but rejects it as not fitting duties to self. In the *Foundations* he substitutes "responsibility" for "prima facie duty." But that terminology never caught on.

Moreover, he at least partly changed his mind about how to characterize the key concept. As we saw in the passages previously quoted, in *The Right and the Good* he characterizes prima facie duty in two distinct ways in terms of duty proper: as what would be a duty proper in the absence of conflicting prima facie duties (what we can label, following

Jonathan Dancy, the "isolation account") and as *tendencies* to be a duty proper (following Dancy again, call this the "tendency account").[3] By contrast, in the *Foundations* he adopts and amends Broad's alternative idea (found in the passages I have quoted) that prima facie duty should be characterized in terms of fittingness, not in terms of duty proper:

> It seems to me that [Professor Broad] should make rightness depend not on a joint consideration of fittingness and utility, but on a joint consideration of fittingness arising from utility and fittingness arising from other sources, such as that a promise has been made. I feel, myself, no difficulty in recognizing, in the tendency which an act has . . . to produce maximum good, something in virtue of which that act tends to be fitting to the situation. (F 81)

But he does not straightforwardly give up on the earlier tendency account; he talks in terms of forces and tendencies soon afterward, on page 84 of the *Foundations*.

Further important questions about definition and theoretical structure were then raised by a number of mid-twentieth-century critics. Some of their criticisms were quite pointed. In an article published in 1963, H. J. McCloskey observed,

> Ross's discussion of *prima facie* duties . . . [is] obscure, confused and inconsistent . . . [and] suffers from the basic defect that Ross attempts to account for the nature of these *prima facie* duties by reference to absolute duties.[4]

And in a celebrated discussion from 1978, John Searle wrote,

> The discussions I have seen of [the notion of a prima facie obligation] . . . are extremely confused. Some, though by no means

all, of the confusion is due to Ross. . . . I shall not spend much space on Ross's account, because it does not seem to me that it can be made consistent internally.[5]

I shall argue first that these verdicts are too harsh. I don't deny that Ross's characterizations of prima facie duty are often problematic or at best partly true. Nor do I deny that he sometimes fails to appreciate the full significance of his key conceptual innovation. But, unlike critics like McCloskey and Searle, I think that he has a clear and plausible theoretical picture nonetheless.

Ross lays out this theoretical picture towards the end of chapter 2 of *The Right and the Good*:

> We may try to state . . . the universal nature of *all* acts that are right. It is obvious that any of the acts that we do has countless effects, directly or indirectly, on countless people, and the probability is that any act, however right it may be, will have adverse effects . . . on some innocent people. Similarly, any wrong act will probably have beneficial effects on some deserving people. Every act, therefore, viewed in some aspects, will be *prima facie* right, and viewed in others, *prima facie* wrong, and right acts can be distinguished from wrong acts only as being those which, of all those possible for the agent in the circumstances, have the greatest balance of *prima facie* rightness, in those respects in which they are *prima facie* right, over their *prima facie* wrongness, in those respects in which they are *prima facie* wrong. (RG 41)[6]

The theoretical picture Ross here lays out contrasts sharply with the theoretical picture associated with simple absolutist deontology. It is worth dwelling on the contrast. Consider first a simple absolutist deontology. Suppose there is a possible act P that would be the keeping of a promise. Suppose the absolutist deontology includes a principle: it is your duty to keep a promise. The acts that are duties have two relevant properties; the base property[7] of being of a kind that is duty-making (in this case the property of being the keeping of a promise) and the normative property of being a duty.

Contrast this with Ross's picture developed for a simple two-option case. Suppose there are just two possible acts: P, an act that would be the keeping of a promise, and G, an act that would produce the most good. Suppose the Rossian theory also includes just two relevant principles of prima facie duty: the principle that it is a prima facie duty to keep your promises and the principle that it is a prima facie duty to produce the most good. Unlike simple absolutist deontology, Ross's picture has to include something that comes in degrees: weight or degree of obligatoriness or prima facie rightness, in order to determine, in this case, whether the prima facie duty to keep the promise is weightier than the prima facie duty to produce the most good or vice versa. And, again unlike simple absolutist deontology, there needs to be a principle connecting prima facie duty to duty proper. The principle Ross endorses is that it is your duty proper to do whatever act there is most prima facie duty to do. It thus involves (as Ross says explicitly in the preceding passage) first considering all possible acts and determining which of these has the greatest balance of prima facie rightness over prima facie wrongness.

Ross's picture is thus significantly more complicated than simple absolutist deontology in that it includes multiple distinct normatively important properties. As in simple absolutist deontology, each possible act has the base properties named in the principles—in this case, that of being (or not) the keeping of a promise, and of being (or not) the doing of the most good. And, for each of these base properties, there is a consequent normative property. But now this initial consequent normative property has to be scalar: it has to be the property of having *a certain degree* of weight or obligatoriness. And there are then three further normative properties: the property of having a certain degree of overall obligatoriness, which is a property of each possible act that depends on combining[8] the degrees of obligatoriness it has in virtue of each of its normatively significant component base properties; the property of being (or not) more obligatory than any other act, which depends both on its overall degree of obligatoriness and on the overall obligatoriness of each alternative possible act; and the further property of being (or not being) a duty proper, which depends on the property of being more obligatory than any other act and the further principle that it is your duty proper to do whatever act there is most prima facie duty to do.

In the light of these reflections, return to the question of the adequacy of Ross's characterizations of prima facie duty earlier in chapter 2 of *The Right and the Good*. Consider first the claim that

> *"prima facie* duty" . . . [is] . . . the characteristic (quite distinct from that of being a duty proper) which an act has, in virtue of being of a certain kind (e.g. the keeping of a promise), of being an act that would be a duty proper if it were not at the same time of another kind which is morally significant.

What Ross says here is not an adequate characterization of the property of being a prima facie duty, for three reasons. First, whether an act is a duty proper doesn't depend only on the morally significant properties it has. It depends also on the morally significant properties of alternative possible acts. So it is not straightforwardly true that an act that is of only one (positive) morally significant kind is thereby a duty proper.[9] Second, prima facie duties don't matter for the evaluation of an option only when that option has only one morally significant property. As Ross's theoretical picture makes clear, they matter in two different ways in other (much more common) sorts of cases: when there are multiple prima facie duties that together make it the case that one possible act is more obligatory than any other and hence is a duty proper; or when, on the flip side, they are outweighed and the act that is (in some respect) a prima facie duty is not a duty proper. In some of the latter cases (as Ross elsewhere recognizes) an outweighed prima facie duty will still have other normative significance. What Dancy calls the "isolation account" is not an adequate characterization of the property of being a prima facie duty in part because it misses these important roles of prima facie duty, and focuses only on the role of prima facie duties in the rare (or indeed impossible) situations in which there is only a single one. And Dancy also emphasizes a third reason why the isolation account is unsatisfactory: it doesn't capture the idea that prima facie duties come in degrees. In the situation in which there are no other relevant prima facie duties, degree of obligatoriness can be ignored. But in the other (much more usual) situations, degrees of obligatoriness are crucial.

In this passage Ross also says that the characteristic of being a prima facie duty is "quite distinct from that of being a duty proper." Some commentators[10] have criticized this claim too; I am inclined to think it is basically right. The characteristic of being a prima facie duty is the characteristic of having a certain degree of obligatoriness or weight in virtue of being of a single morally significant kind. The characteristic of being a duty proper is, on Ross's picture, quite different: it is a further characteristic that acts have in virtue of having a greater overall degree of obligatoriness than any alternative.

If by saying that the two properties are "quite distinct" Ross meant that the property of being a prima facie duty was not in itself normatively significant he would be wrong. Searle criticizes him in part on this ground. He suggests (81) that on Ross's official view prima facie duties are merely apparent duties. If so, Ross cannot make any proper sense of situations in which duties conflict.

But this is clearly not what Ross meant. It is true that Ross picked the wrong Latinism to name his new concept; he would have been better off with "pro tanto duty" than "prima facie duty."[11] But it is no part of his "official view" of prima facie duties that they are merely apparent. He goes out of his way to stress the reverse: that they are "objective fact(s) involved in the nature of the situation" (RG 20).

Now consider a second claim.

> The property of being a prima facie duty is the property of tending to be a duty proper.

This claim might just be an alternate way of stating the isolation account: an act would be understood to have a tendency to be a duty proper just in that it would be a duty proper if neither it nor any alternative to it were of any other normatively relevant kind. If so, for the reasons already given, the claim would be inadequate as a characterization of prima facie duty. On another interpretation, the claim about tendencies would be equivalent to some statistical claim. One candidate would be the following:

(a) "There is a prima facie duty to keep promises" means
(b) Most acts of keeping promises are right.

Though Ross thinks both (a) and (b) are true, he clearly doesn't think (a) means (b). For it is, though false, perfectly possible that most acts of keeping promises should not be right because in most cases the prima facie duty to keep a promise is outweighed by other competing prima facie duties. And even in this unlikely event, (a) would still be true.

The other and better line of thought closely connected in Ross to the talk of tendencies is the force metaphor: the analogy between prima facie duties and individual forces acting on a body. Each prima facie duty is like an individual force on a body; duty proper is analogous to the motion or acceleration of the body produced by the combination of forces to which it is subject. This comparison is, I think, helpful but problematic. It is helpful in three main ways. First, forces are real features of the physical situation regardless of the direction in which a body ultimately moves. Second, forces, like prima facie duties, come in degrees. Third, forces interact and the final motion of a body depends on the interaction of all the forces to which it is subject; similarly with prima facie duty.

There are also, though, four important respects of disanalogy. In one way the normative case is simpler than the force case: the normative is only one-dimensional, while forces operate in three dimensions. But in two other ways the normative case is more complicated than the force case: the interaction of individual prima facie duties need not be additive, and indeed on Ross's view there are important cases where it isn't; and normative judgment is comparative in that it involves evaluating different options rather than just looking at the forces operating on a single body. Finally, though prima facie duty is importantly analogous to individual forces, duty proper is not analogous to the final motion of a body, even if we stick to one dimension. The final motion of a body even in one dimension is scalar, not all-or-nothing: it is motion (or acceleration) of a certain degree positively or negatively. This is most closely analogous to the overall degree of obligatoriness of a possible act. It is not at all so directly analogous to the property of having a greater degree of obligatoriness than any other possible act. And it is still less directly analogous to the property of being a duty proper (which Ross thinks depends on but is distinct from that of having a greater degree of obligatoriness than any other possible act).

Consider finally Ross's claim that prima facie duty is a parti-resultant attribute and duty proper a toti-resultant attribute. The first half of the claim seems true: that an act has a certain degree of obligatoriness in virtue of possessing a base property seems to depend just on that base property. But the claim that duty proper is toti-resultant is in two main ways more problematic. A first problem is that the degree of overall obligatoriness of an act doesn't depend on all of an act's properties. Many of these (as Ross sometimes explicitly notices, including in the passage where he first introduces the concept of prima facie duty) are on his view normatively inert. So the overall obligatoriness of an option doesn't depend on all its base properties, but instead only on its "morally significant" base properties. Second, the property that depends on all of an act's morally significant base properties is the property of having a certain overall degree of obligatoriness.

But, again, as reflection on Ross's theoretical picture makes clear, this is *not* the property of being a duty proper. We have to distinguish the property of having a greater degree of overall obligatoriness than any other option from the property of having a certain overall degree of obligatoriness. And then we further have to distinguish the property of having a greater degree of overall obligatoriness than any other option from the property of being a duty proper. These latter two properties are in an important sense not toti-resultant. For they depend not only on the degree of overall obligatoriness of this possible act; they depend also on the degree of overall obligatoriness of each possible alternative act.

Much of what Ross says in introducing and explaining the concept of prima facie duty thus is indeed misleading or problematic. But he has a clear and coherent theoretical picture nonetheless. The main source of the problems is, I suggest, his failure fully and consistently to recognize and to take into account the additional complexities entailed by the move from principles of duty proper to principles of prima facie duty—in particular, the complexities involved in having four rather than two distinct kinds of normatively important property in the theoretical picture. But, again, I don't think this shows that there is anything fundamentally wrong with the theoretical picture.

2. ROSS, PRIMA FACIE DUTY, AND NORMATIVE REASONS

If I am right so far, no intractable problems with Ross's theoretical picture were raised by mid-twentieth-century critics.

But a different set of issues arises when we try to understand and relate Ross's claims to those made by many more contemporary moral theorists. As T. M. Scanlon observes at the start of *Being Realistic about Reasons*,

> Contemporary metaethics differs in . . . important ways from the metaethics of the 1950s and 1960s, and even the later 1970s, when John Mackie wrote *Ethics*. . . . In that earlier period, discussion in metaethics focused almost entirely on morality. . . . Today . . . a significant part of the debate concerns practical reasoning and normativity more generally.[12]

Like many other contemporary philosophers, Scanlon here draws a distinction between claims about morality and claims about normative reasons.[13]

As Scanlon and many others see it, the concept of a normative reason is fundamental in that it is both naturalistically and nonnaturalistically irreducible.[14] Scanlon inclines to the further view that all other normative claims can be reductively analyzed in terms of the concept of a reason. These views of Scanlon's are far from universal. Some philosophers want to reject and others to reductively analyze the concept of a normative reason.[15] But at least among those who embrace the concept of a normative reason, Scanlon's views about its character and fundamentality are widely shared.

By contrast, though many philosophers distinguish claims about morality from claims about normative reasons, there is considerably less agreement about how to understand the distinctively moral and its relation to the generically normative. One possibility is to identify the moral as a subspecies of the normative with a distinctive substance or content. Michael Smith articulates a view of this kind in *The Moral Problem*:

> What the analysis of normative reasons quite generally leaves out of account—and rightly so, of course—is the distinctive *substance* or *content* of reasons that makes them into moral reasons as opposed to non-moral reasons. The fact that there is such a distinctive substance or content is . . . evident from the platitudes concerning substance that we find amongst the platitudes constitutive of the moral. These are platitudes like "Right acts are often concerned to promote or sustain or contribute in some way to human flourishing," "Right acts are in some way expressive of equal concern and respect," and the like.[16]

Another possibility is to understand moral claims as claims about the rationality of distinctively moral emotions, as Allan Gibbard does:

> What a person does is *morally wrong* if and only if it is rational for him to feel guilty for doing it, and for others to resent him for doing it.[17]

As Gibbard notes, the roots of this conception of morality go at least as far back as Mill.[18] Indeed Stephen Darwall traces it much further back, to the early modern natural lawyers. And Darwall articulates the conception in a distinctive and influential way:

> The concept of moral obligation is conceptually tied to that of moral responsibility or accountability. It is a conceptual truth that what we are morally required or obligated to do, what it would be wrong for us not to do, is what we are warrantedly held accountable for doing and blamed for not doing if we omit the action without a valid excuse. Moral philosophers

from Grotius on made a fundamental distinction between legitimate demands, on the one hand, and rational "counsel" on the other, and placed moral obligations squarely on the demand side of the ledger.[19]

A further influential approach is Scanlon's. He understands the core of morality, what we owe to each other, as involving a distinctive and important subclass of reasons defined in terms of hypothetical agreement:

> What we need to do . . . is to explain . . . how the idea that an act is wrong flows from the idea that there is an objection of a certain kind to people's being allowed to perform such actions, and we need to do this in a way that makes clear how an act's being wrong in the sense described can provide a reason not to do it. . . . Contractualism offers such an account. It holds that an act is wrong if its performance under the circumstances would be disallowed by any set of principles for the general regulation of behavior that no one could reasonably reject as a basis for informed, unforced general agreement.[20]

Ross makes no such distinction between morality and reasons. His unitary concept of duty blends the generically normative with the distinctively moral. Indeed, as I shall now argue, Ross does not possess the contemporary concept of a normative reason. To see this, consider a striking contrast between Ross's views and Parfit's. At the very start of *On What Matters* Parfit introduces the concept of a normative reason. Since it is indefinable, it cannot be explained by giving a definition. Instead, Parfit says

> We must explain . . . concepts [like "a reason"] in a different way, by getting people to think thoughts that use these

concepts. One example is the thought that we always have a
reason to avoid being in agony. (OWM 1, 31)

Parfit's appeal to this thought at this point suggests that he
thinks one of the clearest and most compelling examples of a
reason is the reason to avoid pain for oneself.

In a starkly contrasting passage, Ross writes,

> That we are conscious of no duty to maximize pleasure for our-
> selves seems to be so clear as not to need argument; and per-
> haps what is needed is rather some explanation of why the fact
> has been so much overlooked in ethical theory; it certainly is
> not overlooked in our natural thinking.... Perhaps only a gen-
> eration for which the view that we should seek *only* our own
> pleasure is already out of date can see clearly that we are under
> no obligation to pursue our own pleasure at all. (F 273–74)

Ross focuses here on the positive, pleasure, while Parfit focuses
on the negative, pain. But Ross also thinks that we are under no
obligation to avoid pain for ourselves. This comes out clearly
in a passage a bit later in the *Foundations*. He writes:

> We are never conscious of a duty to get pleasure or *avoid pain*
> for ourselves, as we are conscious of a duty to give pleasure to
> or *prevent pain* for others. (F 277, italics added)

That is, I take it, the difference between Parfit and Ross can
be captured like this:

Ross: We never have a prima facie duty to avoid pain
        for ourselves.[21]
Parfit: We always have a reason to avoid pain for
        ourselves.

There are two possible ways to understand this difference. On one interpretation Parfit and Ross here share the same concept—"prima facie duty" and "reason" are just different names for this shared concept—and the difference between them is a substantive difference in opinions about what reasons or prima facie duties we have. On the other interpretation Parfit and Ross do not here share the same concept—Ross's term "prima facie duty" refers to a different concept than Parfit's term "reason"—so the difference here between Parfit and Ross is conceptual rather than substantive.

The latter diagnosis seems to me clearly right. To see why, notice first how radical Ross's substantive view would be if he were using the same concept as Parfit. Ross would not merely be denying that we have any *special* reason to avoid pain for ourselves; he would be denying that we have *any reason whatever* to avoid pain for ourselves. Other people's pains and pleasures would give us reasons for action; but our own pains and pleasures would give us no reasons for action. It would surely be exceptionally uncharitable to attribute such a view to Ross. Then, second, notice that there is a way (on which we have already drawn) to illuminate the difference between Ross's fundamental concept and Parfit's. Parfit's concept of a normative reason is, as Gibbard puts it, flavorless. It can be alternately expressed by talking about what makes sense. By contrast, Ross's fundamental concept is morally loaded; it is naturally expressed (as Ross himself does) by talking about "duty" and "obligation." Ross denies that we have a *moral duty* to avoid pain for ourselves; Parfit thinks we always have a *normative reason* to avoid pain for ourselves. These claims do not straightforwardly conflict because they employ different fundamental concepts.

My claim that Ross did not possess the contemporary concept of a normative reason is liable to remind the reader of controversial claims Parfit himself makes to the effect that many more recent moral philosophers lacked the concept.[22] So I need to be clear that my claim about Ross differs in an important way from Parfit's claim about later philosophers like Hare, Brandt, and Williams. Parfit's claim about those philosophers is that they lacked the concept of a kind of truth that provides the best answer to normative questions. I do not suggest that Ross lacked the concept of a normative reason in this way. He had a concept of a kind of truth that provides the best answer to normative questions. But it was not the concept of a normative reason because it was morally loaded rather than flavorless.

I shall now argue that this omission is a defect; we should include the concept of a normative reason in our conceptual scheme. One reason to do so, in a book of this kind, is that unless we do we will have trouble understanding the relation between Ross's central claims and important related claims made by contemporary moral philosophers. But there are also independent considerations. If Scanlon and others are right, of course, all normative claims involve the concept of a normative reason; it is a concept that is both fundamental and unavoidable. But it may also help to argue more specifically that it is a concept we need to frame important normative questions. Unsurprisingly, some of these important questions are in the ballpark of the difference between Ross and Parfit we just discussed, questions raised by Sidgwick and others about egoistic and agent-relative reasons. In introducing some of these questions, Parfit writes

> Objective theories also differ in their claims about whose well-being we have reason to promote. . . . According to

> *Rational Egoism*: We always have most reason to do whatever would be best for ourselves.

According to

> *Rational Impartialism*: We always have most reason to do whatever would be impartially best.

. . . In his great, drab book *The Methods of Ethics*, Sidgwick qualifies and combines these two views. According to what Sidgwick calls

> *the Dualism of Practical Reason*: We always have most reason to do whatever would be impartially best, unless some other act would be best for ourselves. In such cases, we would have sufficient reasons to act in either way. . . .

Of these three views, Sidgwick's, I believe, is the closest to the truth. (OWM 1, 130–31)

These are important questions. They cannot be properly raised in a conceptual framework like Ross's that has the concept of moral obligation but not the concept of a normative reason. So we should in this respect revise Ross's conceptual framework; we should adopt a conceptual framework that includes the concept of a normative reason.

We then face the question how to understand Ross's most important normative claims. Any such understanding will inevitably be revisionary. Once we introduce the contemporary concept of a normative reason and distinguish, as Ross did not, between claims about morality and claims about normative reasons, we will inevitably be reframing his views. The two simplest revisionary possibilities are to reinterpret Ross so as to make his central claims claims about normative reasons; or to reinterpret him so as to distinguish claims about morality from claims about normative reasons, and to make his central claims about morality. The first possibility makes "prima facie duty" equivalent to "normative reason" and "duty proper" equivalent to "required by reason"; the second possibility makes prima facie duties right-making features, and duty proper a matter of distinctively moral obligation.

The first option seems to me clearly preferable. It involves no further interpretive difficulties beyond those involved in revising Ross's conceptual scheme (as we should) to include in it the concept of a normative reason. By contrast, if we revise Ross so as to interpret his central claims as claims about morality, we then need to decide among competing conceptions of the distinctively moral, on which matter (in the nature of the case) nothing in Ross is likely to help us.

There is however one version of the idea that Ross's claims are about the distinctively moral that can avoid these difficulties—the kind of idea that Smith articulates, that moral reasons are a subclass of normative reasons distinguished by their content. Indeed, though Ross himself of course does not offer a way of distinguishing moral from nonmoral reasons by content, there is a version of the idea that can be grounded in his writings: the idea that moral reasons are *unselfish* reasons.

To see that this idea has a textual grounding, we can argue that important features of Ross's thinking can be explained by attributing to him what we can call "the selfishness constraint." The general idea of the selfishness constraint is that the moral and the selfish are contraries. It helps make sense of various features of Ross. Consider his treatment of the moral value of motives. In that treatment, the value of motives is largely determined by the value of their objects: a desire for something that is better is a better desire, a desire for something worse a worse desire. But there is an important apparent exception:

> We are convinced that the desire of an innocent sensual pleasure [for oneself] is morally indifferent. (RG 162)

As we will see at considerable further length in chapter 4, Ross's treatment of the question what things are good is to a significant extent driven by an attempt to make sense of this exception. But he fails to notice an obvious way to explain it. The explanation will be that there are two independent determinants of the moral value of different motives. One is responsiveness to normative considerations: a desire for something better is a better desire; the other is that selfish desires are morally valueless. That a desire for one's own pleasure is morally valueless does not mean that one's own pleasure is not good; what makes the desire morally valueless is that it is selfish, not that its object is valueless.[23]

Thus there are independent reasons to attribute the selfishness constraint to Ross. And once we have done so, the selfishness constraint supplies an obvious way, with a Rossian pedigree, to distinguish moral from nonmoral reasons by their content. Moral reasons are a subset of reasons with a distinctive content: they are *unselfish* reasons.

Whichever of these options we adopt—whether we frame Ross's view simply in terms of normative reasons, or distinguish a subclass of moral reasons with distinctive content—this introduction of the contemporary concept of a normative reason is the most important revisionary element in my reading of Ross. It is also, I believe, the matter on which I most disagree with Thomas Hurka's splendid treatment of

Ross and his interlocutors in *British Ethical Theorists from Sidgwick to Ewing.* Hurka discusses deontic concepts on pages 25–33 and would clearly reject my arguments and conclusions. I have some difficulty integrating two different elements of his discussion which seem to me to be in tension with one another. On the one hand, Hurka is officially committed to the view that there is no substantive issue as to whether Ross's concept of prima facie duty is equivalent to the contemporary concept of a normative reason; but one cannot help suspecting that he is tempted by the alternative idea that there is a real difference between the contemporary conceptual scheme and Ross's, and that Ross's conceptual scheme is superior.

So, then, on the one hand, Hurka suggests that "the issue [as to whether the single 'ought' is the 'moral' ought] is really just terminological, and has no substantive implications" (28). To say this is to say that there is no real difference between Ross's concept of prima facie duty and the contemporary concept of a normative reason. I take myself to have provided strong evidence to the contrary: Many contemporary philosophers sharply distinguish normative reasons from moral duties; Ross himself did not possess the contemporary concept of a normative reason; but we should include the concept in our conceptual scheme.

On the other hand, a bit later on pages 31–33, Hurka attacks the contemporary concept of a normative reason. The attack is framed as an attack just on the language of normative reasons, on the assumption that the issue is just terminological. But the passage rather suggests by contrast the idea that there is a difference between the flavorless 'ought' and Ross's unitary concept of duty, that the flavorless 'ought' is misconceived, and that Ross's concept of duty is to be preferred. But because Hurka doesn't give up on treating the issue as terminological, the argument he gives for favoring Ross's conceptual scheme over the more contemporary one(s) is only that the language of "reasons" invites confusion between the normative and the motivational.[24]

Nothing in Hurka's discussion, then, seems to me to undermine the case for a revisionary reframing of Ross's key claims as claims about normative reasons. This revisionary reframing will be important in chapter 3 as we explore Ross's critique of consequentialism. For it will turn out that the most important nonconsequentialist moral reasons that Ross emphasizes are structurally identical to the nonmoral agent-relative reasons that Sidgwick and others recognize. Both kinds of reasons can be defended from consequentialist criticisms in the same way; and the recognition of one class of reasons with this structure supports the recognition of another class of reasons with the same structure. Before we turn to these issues, though, there are two further conceptual matters that require discussion.

3. SCALAR DEONTOLOGY

If I have been right in the previous two sections, Ross's views ought to be reframed in terms of (the contemporary concept of) normative reasons. And the way to do this is either simply to identify prima facie duties with normative reasons without giving any further role to the concept of morality, or to identify prima facie duties as a subclass of normative reasons with a distinctive content: unselfish reasons.

But that does not exhaust the important issues about theoretical structure. We still need to ask how to understand the relation between the contributory and the overall: whether Ross is or ought to be a scalar deontologist. Though the term "scalar deontology" is fairly recent (coined, I think, by Jonathan Dancy), the idea that Ross is or should be a scalar deontologist has a much longer history. For it was suggested, in effect, by Prichard in a number of letters to Ross written just after the publication of *The Right and the Good*. In the one such letter so far published, Prichard concludes,

> The truth is that the more I consider it the less I can make sense out of "*the* act which I am bound to do"—as distinct from "*an* act which I ought to do"—and the more I get to think that the only fact corresponding to the phrase is "the act which I ought to do more than I ought to do any other," and that your "a prima facie" duty is really a duty, your "my duty sans phrase" is, really[,] that of a man's duties which he most ought to do, i.e. that so far as these phrases can be made to stand for facts these must be the facts.[25]

There is clearly some important parallel between what Prichard here suggests as the way to make sense of Ross and the scalar utilitarianism Alastair Norcross has recently advocated. As Norcross characterizes his view,

> Utilitarianism should not be seen as giving an account of right action, in the sense of an action *demanded* by morality, but only as giving an account of what states of affairs are good and which actions are better than which other possible alternatives and by how much. The fundamental moral fact about an action is how good it is relative to other available alternatives. Once a range of options has been evaluated in terms of goodness, all the morally relevant facts about those options have been discovered. There is no further fact of the

form "x is right," "x is to-be-done," or "x is demanded by morality."[26]

Indeed, it is easy to characterize a possible scalar deontology modeled on Norcross's scalar utilitarianism. To make it a scalar *deontology* we need simply to allow that the amount of reason to do an action is not determined only by the goodness of states of affairs:

> Deontology should not be seen as giving an account of right action, in the sense of an action *demanded* by reason, but only as giving an account of what states of affairs are good and which actions there is more reason to do than which other possible alternatives and by how much. The fundamental normative fact about an action is how much reason there is to do it relative to other available alternatives. Once a range of options has been evaluated in terms of how much reason there is to do them, all the normatively relevant facts about those options have been discovered. There is no further fact of the form "x is right," "x is to-be-done," or "x is demanded by reason."

To explore the parallels and the case for interpreting Ross as a scalar deontologist, we can distinguish four possible views about the connection between facts about how much reason there is to do an act relative to other available alternatives and facts about the rightness of action. The most severely scalar view we might label *eliminativist scalar deontology*. According to it, we should reject all talk about the rightness of actions, and talk simply about how much reason there is to do an act relative to other available alternatives. A less austere view we might label *reductive scalar deontology*. According to it, we can talk about the rightness of actions, but claims about the rightness of actions must all be definable in terms of claims about how much reason there is to do an act relative to other available alternatives. A third alternative would no longer be a form of scalar deontology. According to it, there *are* further facts about the rightness of actions. But these further facts are all *determined* by facts about how much reason there is to do an act relative to other available alternatives. A fourth and final alternative is still more distant from scalar deontology. According to it there are further *and independent* facts about the rightness of actions; facts about the rightness of actions not determined by facts about how much reason there is to do an act relative to available alternatives.

The parallels between the case for scalar utilitarianism and the case for scalar deontology may, indeed, be developed further. For the move from ordinary to scalar utilitarianism and the move from absolutist deontology to an ethics of prima facie duty have similar philosophical motivations: to avoid a standard objection. Thus the move from ordinary to scalar utilitarianism is designed to allow the utilitarian to avoid the objection that utilitarianism is too demanding; and the move from absolutist deontology to an ethics of prima facie duty is designed to allow the deontologist to avoid the objection that deontology is rendered incoherent by conflicts of duty.

The question then is how exact the parallels are. I think there is an important difference. To avoid the demandingness objection by going scalar, the utilitarian needs to adopt one of the two scalar alternatives, eliminativist or reductive scalar utilitarianism. Otherwise the demandingness problem is not solved: one option will be right, and this will not just be a matter of how good it is relative to other options. By contrast, to avoid the incoherence objection by introducing the concept of prima facie duty, the deontologist can adopt any view other than that there are further *and independent* facts about rightness. So long as conflicts of duty are understood as conflicts of prima facie duty, and duty sans phrase is determined by what there is more prima facie duty to do, the incoherence objection has been met. Ross's main explicit motivation for adopting an ethics of prima facie duty, that is, does not require him to be a scalar deontologist.

Is there some other reason, perhaps implicit in Prichard, for Ross to adopt scalar deontology? The obvious suggestion is that such a further reason will be a matter of simplicity or conceptual economy. But, though simplicity or conceptual economy does matter, it is hard to see why it would be decisive in this case. As Ross himself remarks in another connection,

> Loyalty to the facts is worth more than a symmetrical architectonic or a hastily conceived simplicity. (RG 23)

If, like Ross himself, one takes it to be a part of ordinary moral thinking that there are facts about what is right which are not simply facts about what there is more reason to do than any available alternative, a generic presumption in favor of theoretical simplicity seems insufficient to justify jettisoning this ordinary belief. Ross is not a scalar deontologist; and there is no compelling reason why he ought to be a scalar deontologist.

It might be urged that there remains an important question which I have not squarely or fully addressed: which of prima facie duty and duty proper is for Ross prior or more fundamental? To the question pressed this way, I think the best response is to distinguish different kinds of priority or fundamentality and to offer a mixed verdict.

One kind of fundamentality is what we can call "conceptual fundamentality": a matter of which of prima facie duty and duty proper is definable in terms of the other. Though Ross himself focuses a good deal in general on questions of conceptual fundamentality, he does not—because of the novelty of the concept of prima facie duty he has just introduced—ask entirely explicitly whether it is definable in terms of duty proper or vice versa. I take it that his tacit view is that duty proper is conceptually fundamental and prima facie duty definable in terms of it. But I don't think that, on reflection, this is the view he should hold. Our earlier conclusions suggest to me that the right view instead is that neither duty proper nor prima facie duty is conceptually fundamental. Specifically, if, as I just argued, Ross neither is nor ought to be a scalar deontologist, then he does not and should not think that duty proper is definable in terms of prima facie duty. And if, as I argued in section 1, none of his characterizations of prima facie duty in terms of duty proper is adequate, then he should not think that prima facie duty can be defined in terms of duty proper either.

A second kind of fundamentality is what we can call "metaphysical fundamentality": it is a matter of which truths, truths about prima facie duty or truths about duty proper, metaphysically determine or make true truths of the other class. Here I think it is truths about prima facie duty that are metaphysically prior. This I think is one implication of the theoretical picture associated with an ethics of prima facie duty as contrasted with the theoretical picture associated with a simple absolutist ethics that I drew on in section 1.

A third kind of fundamentality is what we can call "epistemic fundamentality." It is plausible that if truths about prima facie duty are metaphysically prior to truths about duty proper, then judgments about prima facie duty will be epistemically prior to judgments about duty proper: that we will come to know or believe claims about duty proper on the basis of knowing or believing claims about prima facie duty. I take it that this is Ross's view, but that it takes a distinctive form. For he consistently denies that judgments about particular acts are normally arrived at by deduction from general principles. As he puts it in the *Foundations*:

> The question may, however, be asked: "Once the general principles have been reached, are particular acts recognized as right by deduction from general principles, or by direct reflection on the acts as particular acts having a certain character?" ... Either would be a possible account of what happens. But when I reflect on my own attitude towards particular acts, I seem to find that it is not by deduction but by direct insight that I see them to be right, or wrong. I never seem to be in the position of not seeing directly the rightness of a particular act of kindness, for instance, and of having to read this off from a general principle. (F 171)

But to deny, as Ross here does, that moral knowledge is reached by deduction from general principles is not to deny that we come to know or believe claims about duty proper on the basis of knowing or believing claims about prima facie duty.

A final kind of fundamentality we might call "practical fundamentality." Practical fundamentality would be a matter of motivation; the question would be whether it is judgments of prima facie duty or judgments of duty proper that play the more basic motivational role. I think duty proper is for Ross motivationally fundamental. Judgments of duty proper are, he thinks, immediately connected to action via a general desire to do our duty.[27] There is no such direct connection between judgments of prima facie duty and action.

4. SUBJECTIVE AND OBJECTIVE RIGHTNESS

Parfit writes:

> Suppose that, while walking in some desert, you have disturbed and angered a poisonous snake. You believe that, to save your life, you must run away. In fact you must stand still, since this snake will attack only moving targets. . . . Some people would say that you do have a reason to run away, which is provided by your false belief that this act would save your life. But if we say that false beliefs can give people reasons, we would need to add that these reasons do not have any *normative force*, in the sense that they do not count in favour of any act. . . . It is better to describe such cases in a different way. . . . In the case of the angry snake, given your false belief that running away would save your life, you have a *merely apparent* reason to run away. (OWM 1, 34–35)

In *The Right and the Good*, Ross took a similar line about rightness:

> Many people would be inclined to say that the right act for me is not . . . that which if I were omniscient I should see to be my duty, but that which on all the evidence available to me I should think to be my duty. But suppose that from the state of partial knowledge in which I think act A to be my duty, I could pass to a state of perfect knowledge in which I saw act B to be my duty, should I not say "act B was the right act for me to

do"? I should no doubt add "though I am not to be blamed for doing act A." (RG 32)

But in the *Foundations*, Ross changed his mind. He was persuaded by Prichard, specifically by Prichard's "Duty and Ignorance of Fact" (in *Moral Writings*) to "hold the opposite opinion, that it is the subjectively right act that is obligatory" (F 148). Ross remarks that

> Professor Prichard's . . . reasoning is so conclusive that I cannot do better than reproduce the main features of his argument. (148)

I shall argue that this opinion as to the cogency of Prichard's reasoning is one of Ross's least impressive philosophical judgments.[28]

In a given situation we can distinguish

(a) The act that is in fact most morally suitable to the situation as it in fact is,

(b) The act that is in fact most morally suitable to the situation as the agent believes it to be,

(c) The act which the agent believes to be most morally suitable to the situation as the agent believes it to be.

(There is a fourth related item missing from this list: the act that the agent believes to be most morally suitable to the situation as it in fact is. I shall forthwith follow Ross in ignoring it.)[29] Parfit and the earlier Ross agree that it is (a) that is most normatively fundamental. The most fundamental normative facts are facts about what there is in fact most reason to do, or what acts are in fact most morally suitable. It is not that (b) or

(c) is irrelevant or without normative interest. They are quite clearly relevant to the assessment of agents. But they are still in an important way secondary. *As* agents (rather than when assessing agents), what we aim to discover and be guided by is (a), not (b) or (c). In this sense (maybe among others) (a) is fundamental.

The argument of "Duty and Ignorance of Fact" will be troubling if it shows that (a) is not normatively fundamental in the way Parfit and the earlier Ross think. I shall claim with great confidence that Prichard's argument fails to show this. I have considerable confidence also in criticizing a number of the details of Prichard's argumentation. I have less confidence about the other things I will say about the argument— about how to understand its overall structure and what it is designed to show.

Begin with the perplexing structural issue. The question Prichard initially raises is

> If a man has an obligation, i.e. a duty, to do some action, does the obligation depend on certain characteristics of the situation in which he is, or on certain characteristics of his thought about the situation? (*Moral Writings*, 84)

Ross puts the initial question like this at the start of Lecture VII of the *Foundations*:

> But the question remains, which of the characteristics— objective or subjective rightness—is ethically the more important, which of the two acts is that which we ought to do. (F 147)

These ways of framing the issue immediately raise clarificatory concerns. On the picture in Parfit and the earlier Ross, both the objectively right and the subjectively right play roles in normative thinking, but it is the objectively right that is primary. Do Prichard and Ross begin by assuming to the contrary that there is only one role to be played here, so that we must choose between subjective and objective rightness? If not, do they assume that "ought" and "obligation" necessarily label the most normatively important role, so that if we are convinced that the subjectively right is what we ought or are obliged to do, we must reject the idea that the objectively right is more normatively important? (In the quotation just given, it seems to me Ross instructively runs together the question what determines what we ought to do and the question which of subjective and objective rightness is ethically more important.)

One way to press these questions is to notice that in a prelude to his main discussion of "Duty and Ignorance of Fact" in the *Foundations*, Ross observes,

> Now it is to be noted that, whereas we cannot seriously say of any one that he ought to have a certain emotion, because we do not think it is in his power to acquire it forthwith, there is no such limitation to the use of the word 'right'. We still call grief the right or fitting emotion in certain situations, for instance, even if we do not suppose the person we are thinking about has it in his power to feel grief in those circumstances. Its fittingness depends solely on the nature of the circumstances and not at all on his capacity or incapacity. Thus while we had to reject the wider use of 'ought' . . . as being a loose use, it is the wider use of 'right' that is the proper use of it; although it must be granted that when we use 'right' of acts, as opposed to emotions, we usually think of them as being in the agent's power to do or to forebear from doing. (F 55)

Using the terminology of this passage, we might say: Suppose that there are indeed two different terms, "ought" and "right," and that "obliged" and "duty" are relatives of "ought" rather than of "right." Suppose that "ought" and its correlates are constrained by features of the agent—what she believes and what is in her power—in a way that "right" is not. Why would any of this lead us to think either that we must choose between thinking in terms of what "right" labels rather than in terms of what "ought" labels, or that what "ought" labels is normatively more important than what "right" labels?

Sidgwick is helpful on this issue. He suggests that there is a normative context in which there is room for a genuine conflict between subjective and objective rightness, but that this normative context is of secondary importance:

> It may still be asked whether it is better in any partic-
> ular case that a man should do what he mistakenly believes
> to be his duty, or what really is his duty in the particular
> circumstances—considered apart from his mistaken belief—
> and would be completely right if he could only think so. The
> question is rather subtle and perplexing to Common Sense;
> it is therefore worthwhile to point out that it can have only a
> limited and subordinate practical application. For no one, in
> considering what he ought himself to do in any particular case,
> can distinguish what he believes to be right from what really
> is so: the necessity for a practical choice between "subjective"
> and "objective" rightness can only present itself in respect of
> the conduct of another person whom it is in our power to in-
> fluence. (ME 207)

If Sidgwick is right here, there is much less room for a conflict between objective and subjective rightness than Prichard
and Ross seem to suppose.

Moreover, even if there were a need to make some fundamental choice between objective and subjective duty, the

arguments Ross follows Prichard in giving for choosing subjective duty are on the whole singularly unimpressive. There
are three main arguments, which may be connected.

The first involves concerns about the possibility of
knowing our duty (with "know" often instructively italicized
by both Prichard and Ross). As Ross articulates the argument,

> The general form of a moral rule . . . in the strict sense . . . will
> take the form, "A man ought to do such an act or acts as will
> cause a thing of the kind A to assume a state of the kind
> x" . . . In order to know that some moral rule is applicable to
> me here and now, I must know (a) that the situation contains
> a thing of the kind A capable of having a state of the kind x
> effected in it, and (b) that it is such that some act that I can
> do would cause this A to assume a state of the kind x. Now
> (a) is not always fulfilled. . . . And (b) is *never* fulfilled; I never
> *know* nor can come to *know* that some state that I can bring
> about will produce an effect of the kind x, though I can have
> reason to *think* it. Thus if duty be such as the objective theory
> conceives it to be, I can never know that I have any particular
> duty, or even that any one has ever had or will ever have a duty.
> (F 148–50)

The argument here seems to be

(1) It must be possible to know what is our duty,
(2) On the objective view, it is not possible to know what
     is our duty, so
(3) The objective view is mistaken.

The argument is quite unconvincing. Premise (2) holds
only given Ross's and Prichard's very high standards for
knowledge. For them, knowledge requires certainty.[30] On

familiar alternative conceptions of knowledge as something like justified true belief, premise (2) is false. So one way to respond to the argument is to reject premise (2). Alternatively, suppose we accept Prichard's and Ross's standards for knowledge, and therefore endorse premise (2). Then we should reject premise (1). The most we should insist on is that it be possible to have justified true belief (or, in terminology Ross sometimes uses, "right opinion") as to what our duty is. Third, even setting these difficulties aside, the argument really does nothing to undermine the moral or normative importance of objective rightness; the most it does is to suggest a constraint on the ordinary term "duty": that because it must track something wholly internal to the agent's psychological state or wholly within the agent's control, it cannot track objective rightness. But that does nothing to undermine the idea that objective rightness has just the kind of normative importance that Parfit and the earlier Ross think it has.

A second argument concerns situations involving risk. Prichard's example is a driver deciding whether to slow down before turning from a side road onto a main road. We think the driver ought to slow down; but if in fact there is no traffic on the main road, the objectively right action is not to slow down; so what the driver ought to do is not what is objectively right.

Like the knowledge argument, this argument seems to depend crucially on a controversial epistemic premise. In this case, the premise is that there is no such thing as objective probability or risk; so what is objectively right cannot be partly determined by risk. And as with the earlier argument, the obvious response is two pronged. On the one hand, we can reject the controversial epistemic premise. If so, risk is among the objective features of the situation and so will partly determine what it is objectively right for the driver to do. On the other hand, we can accept the controversial epistemic premise. But if we do that, we can more comfortably also accept that it isn't the case that the driver ought to slow down.

A third argument, which may or may not be independent of the knowledge argument, involves an appeal to blameworthiness. As Ross puts it,

> There is another consideration which tends to show that it is what is right [in the sense of being what the agent thinks to be morally most suitable in the circumstances as he takes them to be] that we think an agent is obliged to do. The notion of obligation carries with it very strongly the notion of the non-discharge of an obligation as blameworthy. Now suppose that of two men one does that which he mistakenly believes to be his objective duty, and the other does that which is his objective duty, believing it not to be so, we should regard the former as at least less blameworthy than the latter. (F 163)

The obvious response is articulated by Ross himself earlier in the lecture. There, in laying out the view he believed when he wrote *The Right and the Good*, he suggests that we can deal with this sort of argument by distinguishing judgments as to the rightness of acts from judgments as to the goodness of agents.

The main arguments Prichard and Ross give for choosing subjective rather than objective rightness seem to me wholly unpersuasive. But, as above, the bigger issue is why Prichard and Ross suppose a choice has to be made. Ross is happy throughout his discussion to allow that there are different senses of 'right' and that what is objectively right is indeed right in one perfectly legitimate sense. But he seems to assume that 'ought' and 'obligation' can have only one sense, and that what is right in this sense is more important than what is right in other senses. I see no strong reason to accept the first assumption, and no reason whatever to accept the second.

Thus the arguments of "Duty and Ignorance of Fact" and of Lecture VII of the *Foundations* on reflection do nothing to undermine the central conclusion of this chapter: that Ross's basic normative claims should be understood (to use some apt words of Sidgwick's) as claims about "valid ultimate reasons for acting" (ME 78). We turn in the next chapter to the question: what prima facie duties are there? What does Ross think are valid ultimate reasons for acting, and is he right?

NOTES

1. Rashdall writes: "The strongest part of Sidgwick's great work consists in its analysis of common-sense Morality. The loose statements of Intuitionists as to the clearness, certainty, adequacy, and self-evidence of the ordinarily received rules of conduct have never been subjected to so searching, so exhaustive, and so illuminating an examination. That task has been done once for all, and need not in detail be done over again." (Hastings Rashdall, *The Theory of Good and Evil*, vol. 1 (Oxford: Oxford University Press, 1907), 83. By contrast recent writers who are less convinced include Thomas Hurka, Robert Shaver, and myself. For Hurka see "Sidgwick on Consequentialism and Deontology: A Critique," *Utilitas* 26.2 (June 2014): 129–52 and *British Ethical Theorists from Sidgwick to Ewing* (Oxford: Oxford University Press, 2014), chapter 7. For my version of a similar critique see *Sidgwickian Ethics* (New York: Oxford University Press, 2011), chapter 4. For Shaver, see "Sidgwick's Axioms and Consequentialism," *Philosophical Review* 123.2 (April 2014): 173–204.

2. A. C. Ewing, *Second Thoughts in Moral Philosophy* (London: Routledge and Kegan Paul, 1959), 126.

3. See Jonathan Dancy, "More Right than Wrong," in Mark Timmons and Robert N. Johnson, eds., *Reason, Value, and Respect: Kantian Themes from the Philosophy of Thomas E. Hill Jr.* (Oxford: Oxford University Press, 2015), 101–18 . See also Jonathan Dancy, *Ethics without Principles* (Oxford: Clarendon Press, 2004), chapter 2.

4. H. J. McCloskey, "Ross and the Concept of a *Prima Facie* Duty," *Australasian Journal of Philosophy* 41.3 (1963): 336.

5. John Searle, "*Prima Facie* Obligations," in Joseph Raz, ed., *Practical Reasoning* (Oxford: Oxford University Press, 1978), 81.

6. Kristian Olsen rightly emphasizes this passage in "Ross and the Particularism/Generalism Divide," *Canadian Journal of Philosophy* 44.1 (2014): 56–75.

7. By calling these "base properties" I mean to defer for now the question whether they are natural or factual properties. I take the issue up in discussing David McNaughton and Piers Rawlings' work in chapter 3.

8. Ross himself in various important ways rejects a simple additive model for such combination. I discuss these matters in chapter 3.

9. It might be nonstraightforwardly true if every morally significant feature of any one option necessarily generated a corresponding morally significant feature in every other option. So, for instance, if one option had the morally significant property of being the act that produces the most good, every other option would thereby have the morally significant property of not being the act that produces the most good.

10. Including McCloskey.

11. The improved terminology was introduced by Shelly Kagan. See *The Limits of Morality* (Oxford: Clarendon Press, 1989), 17.

12. T. M. Scanlon, *Being Realistic about Reasons* (Oxford: Oxford University Press, 2014), 1.

13. Philosophers who make this distinction typically take claims about reasons to be fundamental, and claims about morality to be definable partly in terms of claims about reasons. Gibbard, Scanlon, and Smith, inter alia, take claims about morality to be

definable in terms of claims about normative reasons. Among contemporary philosophers I will draw on in this chapter, Parfit is distinctive in taking moral claims to be irreducible to claims about normative reasons. On this, see *On What Matters*, 2 vols., vol. 1 (Oxford: Oxford University Press, 2011), chapter 7. I will refer to volume 1 as "OWM 1" and volume 2 as "OWM 2." Page references will be placed in the text.

14. Scanlon, *Being Realistic about Reasons*, passim, esp. p. 2; T. M. Scanlon, *What We Owe to Each Other* (Cambridge MA: Harvard University Press, 1998), chapter 1.

15. The most celebrated sustained defense of a reductive analysis is Mark Schroeder's *Slaves of the Passions* (Oxford: Oxford University Press, 2007).

16. Michael Smith, *The Moral Problem* (Oxford: Blackwell, 1994), 183–84.

17. Allan Gibbard, *Wise Choices, Apt Feelings* (Cambridge, MA; Harvard University Press, 1990), 42. This is the easiest quotable short formulation of the analysis Gibbard favors. Pages 40–45 are a helpful discussion of the contrast between morality and reason, which Gibbard initially characterizes as a distinction between broad and narrow conceptions of morality.

18. See chapter 5 of *Utilitarianism* (1861).

19. Stephen Darwall, "Morality's Distinctiveness," in *Morality, Authority, and Law: Essays in Second-Personal Ethics*, vol. 1 (Oxford: Oxford University Press, 2013), 6.

20. Scanlon, *What We Owe to Each Other*, 153.

21. Someone might think that Ross's view is that there is a prima facie duty to produce pleasure and avoid pain for ourselves, but that this is always outweighed. This is not my reading of the passages I cite. As I read them, Ross is there denying that we have even a prima facie duty to produce pleasure or avoid pain for ourselves. If further confirmation is needed that this is the correct reading, I would point to what he says a little later on page 277 of the *Foundations*: "The act of seeking pleasure for oneself is not merely not obligatory, but has not even that specific kind of rightness or fitness which is moral fitness. It seems morally entirely colourless."

22. See OWM 2, esp. 290–94 and 410–25 and "Normativity," in Russ Shafer-Landau, ed., *Oxford Studies in Metaethics*, vol. 1 (Oxford: Oxford University Press, 2006), 325–80.
23. Ross does not think of all self-directed desires as selfish. He thinks of the desire for pleasure for oneself as selfish, but not the desire for virtue or knowledge for oneself.
24. I would also deny Hurka's claim on page 28 that all members of the Sidgwick-to-Ewing school have the same single ought. I think Sidgwick's central deontic concept is the flavorless 'ought', while Ross's is not. And, as Stephen Darwall has suggested, one figure in the Sidgwick-to-Ewing school—Ewing—arguably does have a conceptual framework that involves a version of the contemporary distinction between normative reasons and moral obligations.
25. H. A. Prichard, *Moral Writings*, ed. Jim MacAdam (Oxford: Oxford University Press, 2002), 287. Further page references will be placed in the text.
26. Alastair Norcross, "Reasons Without Demands: Rethinking Rightness," in Jamie Dreier, ed., *Blackwell Contemporary Debates in Moral Theory* (Oxford: Blackwell, 2006), 44.
27. In giving this account of moral motivation Ross is in one familiar sense an externalist. That this is his view is explicit on pages 205–6 and 226–28 of the *Foundations*. I think his commitment to this sort of externalism is shallow, in the sense that he could reject it without changing much else in his normative theory. He could, in particular, model his treatment of moral motivation on Sidgwick's treatment without in other fundamental ways altering his view. Sidgwick's (tricky to interpret but more internalist) view is articulated in ME book 1, chapter 3. For discussion and references see my "Sidgwick's Kantian Account of Moral Motivation," forthcoming in Tim Henning and Tyler Paytas, eds., *The Ethics of Sidgwick and Kant* (Routledge).
28. For a more sympathetic treatment of Prichard's line see Hurka, *British Ethical Theorists*, 78–85. I don't, of course, mean here to argue that objectivism is correct: this is a topic about which there is a sophisticated ongoing current debate. I mean only

to argue that Prichard gave Ross no good reason to change his mind.

29. Broad develops a considerably more fine-grained classification scheme on page 146 of *Ethics*, ed. C. Lewy (Dordrecht: Martinus Nijhoff, 1985).

30. I discuss Ross's epistemological views at much more length in chapters 4 and 5.

3

WHAT PRIMA FACIE

DUTIES ARE THERE?

Ross, Agent-Relativity, and the Rejection of Consequentialism

ROSS AND BROAD BOTH PRESENT themselves as developing a view intermediate between consequentialism and absolutist deontology. As Broad puts it

> The rightness or wrongness of an action . . . is a function of its fittingness . . . and its utility. . . . The pure Deontologist would deny that its utility or disutility was relevant to its rightness or wrongness. The pure Teleologist would deny that there is such a relation as direct fittingness or unfittingness, and would make its rightness or wrongness depend entirely on its utility or disutility. Both these extremes seem to me to be wrong, and to be in flagrant conflict with common sense. (*Five Types*, 221)

While expressing some reservations about Broad's terminology, Ross remarks,

> In the main, Professor Broad's view is just that which I wish to advocate, viz. that among the features of a situation which tend

to make an act right there are some which are independent of the tendency to bring about a maximum of good. (F 82)

In *The Right and the Good*, Ross's initial list of prima facie duties, for which he explicitly does not claim "completeness or finality," goes like this:

(1) Some duties rest on previous acts of my own. These duties seem to include two kinds, (a) those resting on a promise or what may fairly be called an implicit promise, such as the implicit undertaking not to tell lies which seems to be implied in the act of entering into a conversation. . . . These may be called the duties of fidelity. (b) Those resting on a previous wrongful act. These may be called the duties of reparation. (2) Some rest on previous acts of other men, i.e. services done by them to me. These may be loosely described as the duties of gratitude. (3) Some rest on the fact or possibility of a distribution of pleasure or happiness (or of the means thereto) which is not in accordance with the merit of the persons concerned; in such cases there arises a duty to upset or prevent such a distribution. These are the duties of justice. (4) Some rest on the mere fact that there are other beings in the world whose condition we can make better in respect of virtue, or of intelligence, or of pleasure. These are the duties of beneficence. (5) Some rest on the fact that we can improve our own condition in respect of virtue or of intelligence. These are duties of self-improvement. (6) I think that we should distinguish from (4) the duties that may be summed up under the title of "not injuring others." No doubt to injure others is incidentally to fail to do them good; but it seems to me clear that non-maleficence is apprehended as a duty distinct from that of beneficence, and as a duty of a more stringent character. (RG 21)

As he goes on to notice, some of the items on this list seem to be basically consequentialist duties. Items (3), (4), and (5) all involve in some way producing goods. Ross's targets include both hedonistic utilitarianism and ideal utilitarianism, and he tends to run together his criticisms of the two views. But it is ideal utilitarianism that he regards as the most important and plausible competing view; and ideal utilitarians can happily admit (3), (4), and (5). So the crucial nonconsequentialist elements in the initial list seem to be (1), (2), and (6).

The importance of (1) and (2)—of duties of fidelity, reparation, and gratitude—to Ross's overall position comes out in two instructive ways. It is brought out in his striking remarks about what is fundamentally wrong with ideal utilitarianism:

> The essential defect of the "ideal utilitarian" theory is that it ignores, or at least does not do full justice to, the highly personal character of duty. If the only duty is to produce the maximum of good, the question who is to have the good—whether it is myself, or my benefactor, or a person to whom I have made a promise to confer that good on him, or a mere fellow man to whom I stand in no special relation—should make no difference to my having a duty to produce that good. But we are all in fact sure that it makes a vast difference. (RG 22)

And he goes on to use for the duties of fidelity, reparation, and gratitude the term "special obligations," which he contrasts with the consequentialist "general obligation" to do as much good as possible:

> The duty of justice . . . with beneficence and self-improvement, comes under the general principle that we should produce as much good as possible. . . . But besides this general obligation there are special obligations. These may arise, in the first place, incidentally, from acts which were not essentially meant to create such an obligation . . . such acts may be of

two kinds—the infliction of injuries on others, and the accept-
ance of benefits from them. . . . And finally there are special
obligations arising from acts the very intention of which, when
they were done, was to put us under such an obligation. The
name for such acts is 'promises'. (RG 27)

As Thomas Hurka notes,[1] compared to later writers it is
striking how much emphasis Ross places on these special
obligations and how little emphasis he places on (6), the duty
of nonmaleficence.

In this chapter I interpret and defend Ross's rejection
of consequentialism and his endorsement of a moderate
nonconsequentialist position. I begin with the question how
to understand the dialectical situation. I argue that Ross is
overly influenced by Moore, who supposes that consequentialism is an analytic or anyway an immediate a priori truth.
Ross is right that these Moorean claims are implausible. But
there is a better, more indirect, strategy of argument for consequentialism. This strategy begins with a weaker claim: that
there is a prima facie (or pro tanto) reason to promote the
good. It acknowledges that there are other apparent prima
facie duties, nonconsequentialist prima facie duties, but
claims that these are all *only* apparent. On full philosophical reflection, *only* the prima facie duty to promote the good
remains.

Though he tends to misrepresent the dialectical situation, I will argue that nonetheless Ross gives good reason to
reject consequentialism. I will focus on what he says about
promises, the special obligations he discusses most fully.
I will claim (introducing a piece of terminology inspired by
Jonathan Dancy for an idea I will argue is clearly in Ross) that
promises are *agent-relative intensifiers* of reasons to promote

goods. I will draw on Sidgwick and on contemporary moral philosophers influenced by him to argue that there are other important kinds of agent-relative intensifiers. And I will argue that, unlike constraints, agent-relative intensifiers are not puzzling or problematic, so to the extent that Ross adds only agent-relative intensifiers to reasons to promote goods, he avoids problems that afflict more familiar versions of deontology.

I will then contrast my reading of Ross as a classical deontologist with Robert Audi's reading of Ross as a value-based intuitionist.[2] Finally I will explore the relationship between classical deontology and Jonathan Dancy's particularism, aiming both to indicate where and why I think the classical deontologist should part company with the particularist and to consider David McNaughton and Piers Rawling's articulation of a view close to classical deontology.[3]

1. CONSEQUENTIALISM AND ITS CRITICS: MOORE, ROSS, AND ARGUMENTATIVE STRATEGY

When Ross argues against consequentialism, his usual target is Moore. This is unfortunate, because Moore's account of the case for consequentialism is problematic.

As Ross plausibly portrays it, Moore's view is that it is self-evident that what produces the maximum good is right. Initially, in *Principia*, Moore held that this consequentialist claim was true by definition. But then he (rightly) came to see that the definitional claim was false: "right" does not mean "maximally productive of good." So he retreated, in *Ethics*, to the view that though "right" does not *mean* "maximally productive of good," it is nonetheless still self-evident that "right" and "optimific" are coextensive; being optimific is the only ground of rightness.

Ross argues against this claim. He argues first that it is not self-evident that the right coincides with the optimific. As he summarizes

> It seems, on reflection, self-evident that a promise, simply as such, is something that *prima facie* ought to be kept, and it does *not*, on reflection, seem self-evident that production of maximum good is the only thing that makes an act obligatory. (RG 40)

The only other possibility he conceives of is that the coincidence between the right and the optimific might be established by enumerative induction, a possibility about which Ross is (rightly, it seems to me) also skeptical.

Following Moore, Ross here misses an alternative and better strategy of argument for consequentialism. The better strategy of argument for consequentialism is two-stage and indirect. The first stage is to argue that productivity of goodness is *a* ground of rightness (a claim with which Ross himself agrees). The second stage is to argue that there are no other genuine independent grounds of rightness: that all the other candidates to be independent grounds of rightness can be shown not to be. This strategy of argument does not involve establishing the truth of the claim that the right and the optimific necessarily coincide in either of the two possible ways Ross envisages (either by seeing that it is self-evident that they coincide, or that the coincidence can be established by enumerative induction). And it is surely a better account of the consequentialist strategy.

This better strategy is articulated in a number of places. In *Ethics*, Broad writes:

> The argument [for utilitarianism] may be put as follows. (a) If I am told that a certain act would be right or would be wrong in a certain situation, it is always reasonable to ask "*Why* is it right, or *why* is it wrong?" . . . (b) One answer which would often be given is of the following kind. You will be told that the act is right because, by doing it, you will be producing as much good or as little evil as you can under the circumstances. . . . (c) Even non-utilitarian moralists, like Ross, admit that this kind of answer is, in many cases, correct. But they hold that, in many cases, a different kind of answer must be given, an answer that makes no reference to the production of good or evil. . . . At this stage the utilitarian . . . tries to show that these other kinds of answer are not ultimate, and that they all depend on the first kind of answer.[4]

And it is the strategy Shelly Kagan employs in *The Limits of Morality*.[5] He begins with the view of the moderate, who accepts that there is a pro tanto reason to promote the good, but holds that this reason is limited in two ways: by options and by constraints. Kagan goes on to argue against options and constraints. So only the (now unlimited) reason to promote the good remains. And a version of the better strategy has recently been attributed to Sidgwick by Robert Shaver.[6]

With this better picture of the strategy of argument for consequentialism comes a better picture of the argumentative burden on the nonconsequentialist. What the nonconsequentialist must show is that some nonconsequentialist prima facie duties survive reflective scrutiny and consequentialist reinterpretation. Though he doesn't have the right picture of the dialectical situation, I shall argue that Ross nonetheless manages to show just this: that he argues persuasively for some important nonconsequentialist prima facie duties. I will begin with Ross's go-to example: promissory obligation.

2. PROMISES AS AGENT-RELATIVE INTENSIFIERS

Sidgwick observes that the obligation to keep promises is the most compelling apparent example of a nonconsequentialist obligation:

> [The duty of fulfilling promises] . . . certainly seems to surpass in simplicity, certainty, and definiteness the moral rules that we have hitherto discussed. Here, then, if anywhere, we seem likely to find one of those ethical axioms of which we are in search. (ME 353)

Ross seems to agree. As we just saw, he makes the existence of special obligations central to his rejection of ideal utilitarianism. And of the three special obligations, he focuses most on the duty of fidelity. It features consistently as the go-to example as he develops his case against ideal utilitarianism (RG 17–18, 32–33, 34–35, 37–39, 42–47). And he remarks at one point,

> I would go so far as to say that the existence of an obligation arising from the making of a promise is so axiomatic that no moral universe can be imagined in which it would not exist. (F 77)

Ross is careful to note that this does not mean he thinks promissory obligations are necessarily *stronger* than other obligations, and that he focuses on them in part because Pickard-Cambridge does so in his sustained attack on *The Right and the Good*:

> The space I have given to discussing the duty of fulfilling promises might lay me open to the suspicion that I attach an undue importance to this duty. I do not think that this is the case. I have discussed it at length, partly because it is a very clear case of a duty which cannot be reduced to that of producing a maximum of good, and partly because the discussion has been forced on me by a particular critic. (F 113)

But neither of these points, I think, tells against the procedure I propose to adopt here: to follow Ross by focusing on promissory obligation in developing the argument against consequentialism.

Since I will be stressing the idea of what I will call agent-relative intensifiers, it makes sense at this point properly to introduce that idea. Begin with the passage where Ross, I claim, develops and endorses the idea that that is what promissory obligations are. He is considering Pickard-Cambridge's objection that, on Ross's view, all promissory obligations should be equally great, but that a promise to attend a dinner party carries much more weight than a promise to attend an at home.[7] Ross considers and rejects one possible response: that the promissory obligation is equal in both cases, but that there are other independent and greater prima facie obligations to attend the dinner party:

> This, however, would not be in my opinion the correct answer. For it divides my responsibility to my host into a responsibility to fulfil a promise + a responsibility to produce good, the first responsibility being of uniform obligatoriness and the second

being more obligatory according as the good to be produced is greater; and that is not how we think about the matter. What we really think is that we have a single responsibility to our friend to confer on him the promised benefit. . . . There appears to be no reason why one who does not take the utilitarian view of promises should consider the bindingness of all promises to be equal. In our natural thought about it, I believe we think of it as being, as it were, a product of two factors. *One* of these is the value of the promised service in the eye of the promisee; we clearly think ourselves more bound not to fail another person in an important matter, than not to fail him in an unimportant one. . . . The *other* factor tending to increase the obligation to fulfil a promise depends on the way in which and the time at which the promise has been made. Anyone would feel that a promise made casually in a moment of half-attention is less binding than one made explicitly and repeatedly. . . . We may then, if we like to put the matter so, think of the responsibility for conferring a promised benefit as being *n* times as great as the responsibility for conferring an exactly similar unpromised benefit, where *n* is always greater than 1, and, when the promise is very explicit, is much greater than 1. It will follow that it is always our duty to fulfil a promise, except where the uncovenanted benefit to be conferred is more than *n* times greater than the covenanted benefit. We are not able to assign a very definite value to *n* in any case, but I believe there is pretty general agreement that *n* is usually great enough to secure that when the alternative advantage to be conferred is not very different in amount, the promised advantage ought to be conferred. (F 100–101)

I hope it will be fairly easy to see why I suggest the term "agent-relative intensifier" for Ross's idea here.[8] That promises are intensifiers (language I borrow from Jonathan Dancy) is explicit in the passage. They multiply (by some variable *n*, always greater than one) the weight of the promise-independent reason to confer a given benefit. That they are agent-relative in one standard sense also seems clear. If two people can confer a given benefit on a third person, and only one of the two has promised the third person to confer that benefit, then it is only the person who made the promise who has a specially weighty—an intensified—reason to confer the benefit. It is also worth noting at this point that seeing promises as agent-relative intensifiers meshes with Ross's strategy of beginning with ideal utilitarianism and arguing that it is not the whole truth. His treatment of promissory obligation seems to presuppose that there are consequentialist reasons to provide benefits; these are, rather explicitly in these passages and elsewhere, the reasons promissory obligation intensifies. In this way the idea of agent-relative intensifiers is a natural part of a view conceived as a compromise between consequentialism and deontology.

It is worth being explicit about the character of Ross's theoretical picture once agent-relative intensifiers are introduced. As we saw in chapter 2, on Ross's view certain facts, like the fact that a possible act will produce a certain amount of good, are morally significant in that they provide reasons or generate prima facie duties. In this chapter we are focusing on an important additional idea. It turns out, I claim, that Ross thinks that some facts are morally significant in a different way: they don't provide self-standing reasons, but instead multiply or intensify prior reasons. As with independent reasons to promote goods, we can distinguish the base property from the normative significance it is supposed to have. But now we should also distinguish two different ways in which base properties can have normative significance: by being independent reasons or by being agent-relative intensifiers of such independent reasons.

In the rest of this section I will draw on Ross to argue somewhat more systematically that promises are agent-relative intensifiers. I will argue that seeing promises this way fits with a number of strong intuitions about promissory obligation—that, to use language Ross at one point employs in the *Foundations* (91), the view that promises are agent-relative intensifiers "squares with the facts of the moral consciousness." Then I will respond to some objections.

The first intuition, emphasized by Ross in *The Right and the Good*, is the intuition that the fact that one made a promise *is* intrinsically morally significant. Ross makes this point in one way early in chapter 2 of *The Right and the Good*, appealing to ordinary moral thinking about easy cases:

> When a plain man fulfils a promise because he thinks he ought to do so, it seems clear that he does so with no thought of its total consequences, still less with any opinion that these are likely to be the best possible. He thinks in fact much more of the past than of the future. What makes him think it right to act in a certain way is the fact that he has promised to do so—that and, usually, nothing more. (RG 17)

While Ross does not immediately reject consequentialist attempts to explain away this intuition, as his sustained engagement with the consequentialist alternative as put forward in particular by Pickard-Cambridge shows, he is right that it is a powerful apparent intuition that the fact that a promise has been made has intrinsic normative importance.

The second such intuition is an intuition about who promises are owed *to*, and thus about the nature of the wrong involved in promise-breaking (or about the nature of the reason not to break promises). The idea is emphasized by Scanlon in setting up his argument against consequentialist and institutional accounts of promissory obligation:

> According to the standard institutional analyses [promissory] obligations arise from a general duty to comply with just and useful social practices. I will argue, however, that the wrong of breaking a promise and the wrong of making a lying promise are . . . moral wrongs which are concerned not with social practices but rather with what we owe to other people when we have led them to form expectations about our future conduct.[9]

Ross argues in very similar ways:

> A promise being this, an intentional intimation to someone else that he can rely upon me to behave in a certain way, it appears to me perfectly clear, that, quite apart from any question of the greatness of the benefits to be produced for him or for society by the fulfilment of the promise, a promise gives rise to a moral claim on his part that the promise be fulfilled. This claim will be enhanced if there are great benefits that will arise from the fulfilment of the promise in contrast to its violation; or it may be overridden if the fulfilment of the promise is likely to do much more harm than good. But through all such variations it remains as a solid fact in the moral situation. (F 77)

The third intuition is one that consequentialists might appeal to in arguing against simplistic deontological accounts of promissory obligation—the intuition that promises to do something important count much more than promises to do something trivial. This is where it begins to matter that promises are treated as agent-relative intensifiers of independent goods or benefits. One of the points Ross makes in the passage I quoted from at length earlier in which (as I want to put it) he introduces the idea of agent-relative intensifiers is that, if promises are agent-relative intensifiers, it will of course be true that promises to do something important carry more normative weight than promises to do something trivial. For, whatever the value of n, n times some very large good will be a more weighty consideration than will n times some relatively trivial good.

The fourth intuition is the one most directly involved in the reply to Pickard-Cambridge on dinner parties and at homes. Treating promises as agent-relative intensifiers is compatible with treating promissory obligations as themselves of varying weight, determined by the seriousness with which the promise is made.

The first two of these intuitions support the idea that promissory obligations have normative weight independent of the good produced by keeping a promise. The latter two support the idea that that normative weight has a specific character—that rather than being independent, stand-alone reasons, promises are agent-relative intensifiers of reasons to promote particular goods.

I am arguing both that Ross thinks that promises are agent-relative intensifiers, and that Ross's account of promissory obligation, so interpreted, is plausible. Both these claims could be questioned.

It is worth first saying a little more about the interpretive issue. The obvious alternative to the agent-relative intensifier interpretation of Ross is an interpretation according to which he thinks promissory obligation is primitive: that there is an obligation of some fixed weight to keep every promise, and that this weight cannot be further analyzed.

I think the interpretation according to which Ross thinks that promissory obligation is primitive fits the texts less well overall than does the agent-relative intensifier interpretation, for two reasons. First, though there are passages where it sounds as though Ross thinks that promissory obligation is primitive, these passages tend to be brief and introductory. The agent-relative intensifier view, by contrast, is, as we just saw, found in the place—Lecture V of the *Foundations*—where he develops his account of promissory obligation most carefully and at most length. Second, the agent-relative intensifier interpretation fits with a good deal of what Ross says about the other two special obligations, the obligations of reparation and gratitude, and thus allows him to give a structurally unified account of the special obligations. Consider for example the following passage

> A benefactor is not only a man, calling for our effort on his behalf on that ground, but also our benefactor, calling for our *special* effort on *that* ground. (RG 30)

This passage surely suggests that the fact that someone is a benefactor functions as an intensifier.

Turn now to the question whether the agent-relative intensifier account of promissory obligation I am attributing to Ross is plausible. Consequentialists would of course reject the account. I cannot here respond to every possible consequentialist criticism. But I do want to say something more about some familiar kinds of criticism.

Consider first a type of criticism that Pickard-Cambridge made and Ross responded to. Pickard-Cambridge presented a number of problem cases. They largely involve significant and unforeseen changes between the circumstances in which the promise was made and the later circumstances in which the question arises as to its bindingness. One illustration will be sufficient to convey both the character of the cases and the contours of Ross's response:

> I promise (a) to call at X's house at 2 p.m. tomorrow and (b) to go for a walk with him. He falls ill so that promise (a) cannot be fulfilled. Mr. Pickard-Cambridge says that on my theory I ought to maintain that promise (a) is still binding. But it is surely perfectly clear that the assumed condition of both promises is that X and I are well enough to go for a walk, and that, this condition being unfulfilled, the *prima facie* obligation to fulfil either disappears. If, on the other hand, the promise to call at his house were independent of the assumed condition that he is well enough to go for a walk, it would still hold good. (F 96)

Ross, that is, plausibly suggests that many such cases cease to be problematic when we remember the (necessarily unexpressed) conditions to which a normal promise is subject.

It might be argued, however, that there are cases that cannot be plausibly treated in this way. Sidgwick writes,

> If we ask (*e.g.*) how far our promise is binding if it was made in consequence of false statements, on which, however, it was not understood to be conditional; or if important circumstances were concealed . . . different conscientious persons would answer these and other questions (both generally and in particular cases) in different ways. (ME 353–54)

If there are genuine problem cases of this kind, cases where conscientious persons are unclear whether there is a promissory obligation and how strong it is even when they take into account the unexpressed conditions to which a normal promise is subject, is Ross's view rendered problematic?

I think it is not. Why should the fact that it is difficult to tell, in some borderline case, whether a promise has been made or is still in effect, show that Ross is wrong in his analysis of promissory obligation in ordinary clear cases? There are difficult borderline cases of many normatively significant concepts—concepts like person, sentience, death. That we are, for example, unclear whether a clam is sentient or whether a one-year-old is a person should not lead us to doubt that sentience and personhood have intrinsic normative significance in ordinary cases; nor, similarly, should the fact that we are unclear in certain unusual circumstances whether a promise is still binding lead us to doubt that promises have intrinsic normative significance in ordinary cases.

At the end of Lecture V of the *Foundations*, the lecture devoted to the sustained articulation and defense of his view on the obligation to fulfill promises, Ross remarks,

> The other principles of duty which, I have suggested, fall outside the utilitarian scheme could be defended by arguments similar to those by which I have defended the independence of the principle of promise-keeping; but it would be tedious to develop such a defense. If I have convinced any one that there is one principle that falls outside the utilitarian scheme, he will probably be ready to admit that there are others also; and if I have not convinced him in this case, I should not be likely to do so in others. (F 113)

I think Ross is right here to this extent: if we are persuaded that promises are agent-relative intensifiers, we will be very liable to be persuaded that the same is true of the other special obligations he discusses, the duties of reparation and gratitude. But the same cannot be said of duties of nonmaleficence—these are not at all clearly special obligations and they do not appear to be structurally analogous to promissory obligations, so if we agree with Ross about promissory obligation we don't seem liable to agree with him about nonmaleficence. I will return to this issue. But first I want to introduce and argue for other important kinds of agent-relative intensifiers which are not recognized by Ross.

3. OTHER AGENT-RELATIVE INTENSIFIERS

As we saw in chapter 2, Ross himself does not distinguish morality from reason. He thus fails to recognize that we have *any* reason to promote pleasure or avoid pain for ourselves. As I argued, the view that we have *no* reason to promote our own pleasure or avoid our own pain is quite implausible.

But there is a further key point. Our own pleasures and pains are not just things we have some reason to be concerned about, as we have with anyone else's pleasures and pains. Instead there are strong intuitive arguments that we have *special* or *extra* reason to be concerned with our own pleasures and pains. If so, our reasons for concern for our own pains and pleasures are importantly analogous to Rossian promissory obligations: like them they involve agent-relative intensifiers.

The intuitive arguments are made, inter alia, by Sidgwick and by Roger Crisp. Pressed to explain the self-evident basis of egoism, Sidgwick writes,

> It would be contrary to Common Sense to deny that the distinction between any one individual and any other is real and fundamental, and that consequently "I" am concerned with the quality of my existence as an individual in a sense, fundamentally important, in which I am not concerned with the quality of the existence of other individuals: and this being so, I do not see how it can be proved that this distinction is not to be taken as fundamental in determining the ultimate end of rational action for an individual. (ME 498)

Sidgwick's main idea in this passage can readily be expressed using the concept of an agent-relative intensifier. The fact that a pain will befall me rather than someone else gives me special extra reason to be concerned with the pain—special extra reason that other people don't have. Facts about personal identity, that is, are agent-relative intensifiers of hedonic reasons.[10]

Crisp advocates a view of this Sidgwickian kind, which he calls the "dual-source view." In developing the dual-source view he sharply distinguishes reasons from values. Values are objective and agent-neutral. And values give rise to reasons—impartial reasons. But

> Even if all *values* are to be assessed from the objective point of view . . . there are certain agent-relative *reasons* which cannot be captured from or grounded in that point of view.[11]

Crisp argues largely by appealing to a series of "two doors" cases. The case which most straightforwardly supports the claim that there are agent-relative reasons to promote your own well-being is Two Doors 3:

> *Two Doors 3.* You are confronted by two doors. If you do not pass through one or the other of them, you will suffer an

extremely painful electric shock. If you pass through door A, you will experience a less painful but significant shock. If you pass through door B, you will not experience this shock, but some other person, a stranger and out of sight, will suffer a shock of the same intensity. . . . Surely you have a reason—a strong reason—to choose door B over door A grounded in the fact that it is that door which will significantly promote your well-being. . . . One's own well-being is indeed part of the whole, in the sense that it is one of the components of the sum total of well-beings at stake. But that is not the whole story. What also determines your reasons is the fundamental fact that your own well-being is yours.[12]

And, as we saw in chapter 2, Parfit too endorses a view of this kind.

Thus, in a way Ross himself fails to recognize, his special obligations are not the only normative phenomena whose structure involves agent-relative intensifiers. Hedonic reasons have the same structure. There are nonmoral agent-relative intensifiers in addition to the moral agent-relative intensifiers for which Ross argues.

And there may be further normative phenomena of the same kind. In "Self and Others," Broad discusses partial reasons putatively derived from special relationships to others of which familial relationships are a familiar and important example. Broad famously calls the view, which he attributes to common sense but does not endorse, "self-referential altruism":

The altruism which common sense approves is always *limited in scope*. It holds that each of us has specially urgent obligations to benefit certain individuals and groups which stand in special relations to *himself*, e.g. his parents, his

children, his fellow-countrymen, etc. And it holds that these
special relationships are the ultimate and sufficient ground for
these specially urgent claims on one's beneficence.[13]

I will not here take any position on whether these
relationships do provide further agent-relative intensifiers.
Instead I will claim only that personal identity is an agent-
relative intensifier of hedonic reasons. The structural
similarities between the view that personal identity is an
agent-relative intensifier of hedonic reasons and Ross's
view that there are special obligations of fidelity, gratitude, and reparation are important. For the arguments for
moral and nonmoral agent-relative intensifiers are mutually reinforcing: once we accept the possibility that consequentialism is mistaken in one way, by failing to allow for
the existence of one kind of agent-relative intensifiers, it is
easier to accept the possibility that it is mistaken in another
way, by failing to allow for another kind of agent-relative
intensifier.

4. THE COHERENCE AND DEFENSIBILITY OF AGENT-RELATIVE INTENSIFIERS

Both (ethical or normative) egoism and standard deontological constraints have been charged with incoherence. In this
section I will argue, following Broad, that the charges against
egoism fail. Hence there is nothing irrational or incoherent
about agent-relative intensifiers. By contrast, as I will go on to
argue in the next section, constraints or absolute prohibitions
are harder to defend. This provides a good reason to make

deontology a matter of agent-relative intensifiers rather than of absolute prohibitions.

Begin with the charges against egoism. Criticizing Sidgwick, G. E. Moore articulates them with characteristic force:

> The only reason I can have for aiming at 'my own good,' is that it is *good absolutely* that what I so call should belong to me—*good absolutely* that I should *have* something, which, if I have it, others cannot have. But if it is *good absolutely* that I should have it, then everyone else has as much reason for aiming at *my* having it as I have myself. If, therefore, it is true of *any* single man's 'interest' or 'happiness' that it ought to be his sole ultimate end, this can only mean that *that* man's 'interest' or 'happiness' is *the sole good, the* Universal Good, and the only thing that anyone ought to aim at. What Egoism holds, therefore, is that *each* man's happiness is the sole good—that a number of different things are *each* of them the only good thing there is—an absolute contradiction! No more complete and thorough refutation of any theory could be desired. (*Principia*, 99)

Broad is unimpressed. One of the points he makes in "Self and Others" is that the charge of incoherence fails:

> An Ethical Egoist . . . can admit that, if a certain experience . . . of *his* own would be intrinsically good, a precisely similar experience . . . of B's would . . . be also and equally good. But he will assert that his duty is not to produce good experiences and good dispositions as such, without regard to the question who will have them. A has an obligation to produce good experiences . . . in A. . . . Similarly, B has an obligation to produce good experiences in B. . . . A can admit this about B, and B can admit it about A. Plainly there is no *internal inconsistency* in this doctrine.[14]

For just the same reason that (what Broad actually labels the "extreme form" of) ethical egoism is not incoherent, the view that there are agent-relative intensifiers as well as agent-neutral reasons is not incoherent. It is no more incoherent to assert that each person has *some special* obligation (or reason) to produce good experiences of his own than it is to assert that the *only* good experiences each person has any obligation (or reason) to produce are his own. Agent-relative intensifiers are not puzzling or incoherent. It is, of course, perfectly reasonable to ask of any fact or relationship proposed as an agent-relative intensifier of a reason provided by a particular sort of good whether it is genuine, or whether the intuitions which seem to support the claim that that fact or relationship is an agent-relative intensifier can be dismissed or can be better explained in other ways. But there is nothing puzzling or problematic about the basic idea of agent-relative intensifiers.

To put this point in a slightly different way: Moore and those who follow him object to egoism and its weaker relatives by claiming that all value is agent-neutral and that the only reasons there are are reasons to promote this agent-neutral value. But this claim is dogmatic and unsustainable. It is perfectly coherent to hold that agent-neutral value gives rise to special agent-relative reasons as well as general agent-neutral reasons. Agent-relative reasons, so understood, are quite coherent and quite intuitive.

5. DEONTOLOGICAL CONSTRAINTS

Contemporary deontological theories (which I will sometimes label "standard deontology") have as their distinctive core not agent-relative intensifiers but deontological constraints. I shall argue in this section that such deontological constraints are fundamentally different from and much harder to justify than the agent-relative intensifiers discussed in sections 3 and 4.

To make the argument I will draw substantially on Shelly Kagan's *The Limits of Morality*. The intellectual geography of Kagan's discussion provides a strikingly illuminating comparison with Ross.[15] Kagan aims to argue against what he calls "ordinary morality" and in favor of a straightforwardly consequentialist position he calls "extremism." The defender of ordinary morality—aka the "moderate"—agrees with the extremist that there is a pro tanto reason to promote the good. But, unlike the extremist, the moderate argues that the pro tanto reason is limited in two important ways: by constraints and by options. Constraints forbid

> various types of acts *even* if the best consequences overall could be achieved only by performing such an act. I may not murder my rich uncle Albert . . . even if this is the only way to guarantee that his millions get spent on famine relief. (*Limits of Morality*, 4)

The other way in which the pro tanto reason to promote the good is limited is by (agent-centered) options:

> On the view of ordinary morality . . . I am permitted to favor my interests, even if by doing so I fail to perform the act which leads to the best consequences overall. (*Limits of Morality*, 3)

The setup of Ross's discussion is strikingly analogous to Kagan's. Ross too admits in effect (what Kagan calls) the pro tanto reason to promote the good. Like Kagan's moderate, Ross adds something. But (most of) what Ross adds is, as we have just seen, agent-relative intensifiers, not constraints or options. My claim, in effect, is that Ross's position is importantly different from and much more plausible than the position of Kagan's moderate.

Kagan argues against the moderate in part by targeting ordinary morality as an overall package, featuring both constraints and options. But he also rehearses and develops independent arguments against constraints. In drawing on that discussion here, I cannot, of course, hope to provide anything close to a definitive argument against constraints. I can hope only, much more modestly, to remind the reader why constraints seem to many philosophers problematic.

Kagan's rejection of constraints has two main elements. One involves a challenge for the defender of constraints strikingly like the challenge Moore raises against egoism: the challenge to justify the agent-relative character of constraints. The challenge is also articulated by Nagel in *The View from Nowhere*.[16] Nagel claims that, unlike reasons of autonomy stemming from the projects and concerns of the agent, and unlike agent-neutral reasons to promote the good, deontological prohibitions are "formally puzzling":

> We can understand how autonomous agent-relative reasons might derive from the specific projects . . . of the agent, and we can understand how neutral reasons might derive from the interests of others, giving each of us a reason to take them into account. But how can there be relative reasons to respect the claims of others? How can there be a reason not to twist someone's arm which is not equally a reason to prevent his arm from being twisted by someone else?
>
> The relative character of the reason cannot come simply from the character of the interest that is being respected, for that alone would justify only a neutral reason to respect the

interest. And the relative reason does not come from an aim or project of the individual agent, for it is not conditional on what the agent wants. Deontological restrictions, if they exist, apply to everybody. (*View from Nowhere*, 198)

In chapter 1 of *The Limits of Morality*, Kagan considers and finds wanting various attempts to meet this challenge. He focuses on an abstractly described case in which by killing one innocent person I can prevent the murders of two other innocent persons. We can sample two of the attempts he considers. One is to appeal to the badness of what is done to the victim. But, as Kagan says,

> The death of my victim is a horrible thing to happen to him; but the deaths of the two other potential victims are obviously horrible things to happen to *them*. . . . Why should I be forbidden to minimize the badness? (*Limits of Morality*, 28)

A second proposal involves the idea of treating a person with respect, as a means not an end. But

> The moderate hasn't shown that treating a person with the respect that is due him requires something *different* from taking his well-being equally into account in weighing the objective value of an outcome and promoting the best outcome overall. (32)

The second element of Kagan's case against constraints involves much more detailed consideration of the most plausible articulations of the view that there is a constraint against harming. It will not be productive to go into the details of his discussion here, much less into the details of the vast literature on the moral significance of distinctions of this kind to

which Kagan contributes.[17] We should just instead recollect
the outlines of the debate. The defenders of familiar contemporary deontological positions (standard deontology) characteristically point to pairs of cases which differ only in some
causal, nonmoral respect (for example that one is a killing
and the other a letting die). They claim, with initial plausibility, that the causal difference seems intrinsically morally
significant (for example, that killing is worse than letting
die). And, if they are defending constraints, they claim that
the moral theoretic result is a constraint (for example, a prohibition on killing). Those on the opposing side offer various sorts of objection. One familiar sort of objection is that
in new and ingenious cases the causal difference lacks the
moral significance it seems to have in the initial case; so the
initial specification of what causal difference had intrinsic
normative significance was mistaken. A second familiar sort
of objection is that the supposed causal difference is not really merely causal: that we turn out to distinguish (e.g.) cases
of killing from cases of letting die in part by appeal to moral
rather than causal differences.

Thus reminded of the debate about constraints, we
should reconsider Rossian special obligations. My central
claim is that they are different from and much more defensible than constraints.

To see this, consider in turn the two elements of Kagan's
case against constraints. The first problem is to explain why
constraints take an agent-relative form; to explain why the
values that might be supposed to ground constraints generate something agent-relative. As we have already seen, the
defender of Rossian special obligations has a convincing response to this kind of challenge. It is not in the least puzzling, and very plausible, that I have special reason to be

concerned with my own pains and pleasures. This special reason derives from a normatively significant fact about the relationship between the agent and the person who will have the experience: personal identity. On the same model, the special obligation to keep a promise derives from a normatively significant fact about the relationship between the agent (the promiser) and the promisee. Similarly, the duties of gratitude and reparation derive from other normatively significant facts about the relationships between agents and other specific agents that are apt to generate agent-relative reasons. It is not formally puzzling that I am bound by my promise to A in a way which means that if I have to choose between conferring a benefit on A and on B I should confer it on A, while if you have to choose you should confer it on B. It is not formally puzzling that I have stronger reason to keep my promise than you have to ensure that I keep my promise. Such agent-relative reasons are no more formally puzzling than the reasons for special concern with one's own happiness or well-being discussed by Sidgwick, Parfit, and Crisp.[18]

The other general sort of problems faced by the defender of constraints are to identify the causal difference between prohibited and nonprohibited action types, to explain why this causal difference is normatively significant, and to explain why it gives rise to a constraint. Here again, I think the defender of Rossian special obligations is on stronger ground than the defender of standard deontological constraints. One way to see this is to ask what the analogue is of the pairs of cases often discussed in debates about standard deontology. As we saw, the standard deontologist's paired cases typically differ causally; they differ as to how some outcome is brought about (e.g. as to whether it involves killing or letting die).

By contrast, as his striking remarks about "the highly personal character of duty" remind us, Ross's main focus is not
on *how* but on *who*. The key issue is not a causal issue as to
whether I directly or indirectly affect P; it is instead whether
P stands in some special relationship to me (promisee, benefactor, victim) which gives me special reason for concern
with P's good. To my mind it is much more plausible that
these differences as to who are intrinsically normatively significant than it is that the standard deontologist's differences
as to how are intrinsically normatively significant.

No doubt a note of caution is in order here. There is a
huge literature on standard deontology. Ross's distinctive
views have been much less discussed. We should therefore
expect problems with the former to have been much more
fully explored than problems with the latter. Perhaps the
claim that the promisee/nonpromisee distinction is intrinsically normatively significant might come to seem as problematic as the claim that the killing / letting die distinction is
intrinsically normatively significant (though I am disposed
to doubt it).

Rossian special obligations, then, are different from
and much more defensible than standard deontological
constraints. We noted earlier how much emphasis Ross
places on these special obligations in distinguishing his view
from ideal utilitarianism. He tends to present his view about
rightness as *just* featuring reasons to promote the good plus
special obligations. Thus, for instance, at the start of Lecture
XI of the *Foundations*, he writes:

> A great part of our duty—indeed, according to a widely ac-
> cepted theory, the whole of our duty—is to bring what is good
> into existence. Even if we reject that theory it must be admitted

> that where no special duty such as that of promise-keeping is involved, our duty is just to produce as much good as we can. (F 252)

And later in the same lecture he remarks,

> It is a widely accepted view that productivity of good is the only duty. I have given reasons for holding that this view is not true—that there are other principles of duty, viz. that of fulfilling promises, that of making reparation for injuries done, and that of making a return for goods received. (F 271)

The view that the only principles of moral duty are productivity of good plus special obligations has significant attractions. It is a view intermediate between consequentialism and absolutist deontology. And it is much less open to objection than familiar alternatives that admit the pro tanto reason to promote the good, like the position of Kagan's moderate. If we interpret Ross as a classical deontologist—as adding only agent-relative intensifiers to the pro tanto reason to promote the good—his is a distinctive and attractive normative theory.

6. ROSS AND THE HARM/ BENEFIT ASYMMETRY

But there is a complication. One item on Ross's list of prima facie duties, nonmaleficence, is not straightforwardly a special obligation and looks more like a weakened variant of a constraint. Even with nonmaleficence included, Ross's moral theory still includes no constraints; that, as we saw in chapter 2, is one important consequence of the framing of his theory in terms of prima facie duties. But Ross's endorsement of nonmaleficence might seem to show that he cannot be interpreted as (simply) a classical deontologist. The question for this section is whether this interpretive claim is correct.

I will argue that it is not. The proper charitable way to interpret Ross, I claim, is not to allow nonmaleficence to introduce a new *kind* of reason into his theory. As we have seen, everything else on his provisional list of prima facie duties is either a duty to promote a good (and so covered by the general obligation to promote the good) or a special obligation (and so an agent-relative intensifier of reasons to promote specific goods). As we have also seen, constraints and their weaker relatives as often understood are neither of these; and, so understood, they raise new and serious philosophical problems. The duty of nonmaleficence is relatively insignificant to Ross. It is not his go-to example of a nonconsequentialist duty; and he often instructively forgets about it when summarizing his view and explaining how his view differs from ideal utilitarianism. This means that it is not charitable to him to understand nonmaleficence as a new and distinctively problematic kind of deontological reason, different both from the obligations to promote goods and from the special obligations. Instead the charitable reading of Ross is to understand nonmaleficence either as a kind of special obligation or as involving an extra intrinsic good. I will consider these options in turn.

It is certainly possible in the abstract to view nonmaleficence as a kind of special obligation. The idea will be that the relationship between me and those I am in a position to harm is morally salient in a way that the relationship between me and those I am in a position to benefit is not; and that this gives me special reason not to harm. Versions

of something like this idea make appearances in the literature on standard deontology, as in the following passage
from Kagan:

> [The] focus of the moderate's argument [may shift] to the *re-*
> *lationship* which obtains between the agent and his victim. . . .
> If I kill my victim, I stand in a particular relationship to him—
> and moderates have stressed how horrible it is for that re-
> lationship to obtain. . . . Presumably I do not stand in these
> horrible relationships with all those whom I merely allow
> harm to befall. (*Limits of Morality*, 28)

But there is, I think, important reason to be skeptical. Is the
relationship between two individuals where one is a possible
harmer of the other really morally salient in a way the relationship between two individuals where one can allow harm
to befall the other is not? If not, nonmaleficence cannot be
understood as a special obligation.

It is more promising, I think, to understand
nonmaleficence as involving an additional higher-order intrinsic good. The strategy of understanding what might
appear to be a nonconsequentialist duty as really a duty to
promote an additional higher-order intrinsic good has an excellent Rossian pedigree. For this is exactly the way in which
Ross himself understands the duty of justice. On his view,
justice is not a matter of a new and distinctive kind of obligation. It is rather a matter of a new kind of higher-order good.
As he says,

> The duty of justice is particularly complicated, and the word
> is used to cover things which are really very different—things
> such as the payment of debts, the reparation of injuries done
> by oneself to another, and the bringing about of a distribution

of happiness between other people in proportion to merit. I use the word to denote only the last of these three. In the fifth chapter I shall try to show that besides the three . . . simple goods . . . there is a more complex good, not reducible to these, consisting in the proportionment of happiness to virtue. The bringing of this about is a duty which we owe to all men alike . . . [it] therefore, with beneficence and self-improvement, comes under the general principle that we should produce as much good as possible, though the good here involved is different from any other. (RG 26–27)

Ross himself, of course, does not employ this same strategy in thinking about nonmaleficence. That is, I think, because he does not recognize how distinctive and distinctively problematic nonmaleficence might otherwise be. But the strategy can nonetheless readily be deployed to understand the distinctive badness of harming or injuring. The extra badness of harming can be seen as an instance of what might well be a more general recursive principle.[19] The recursive principle says that there is additional good when attitudes to base goods have the same valence as the base goods (or bads) themselves; and additional bad when the valence of the attitude is opposite to that of the base good. Thus it is good to desire and be pleased by goods; bad to desire and be pleased by bads. Harming or injuring can then be understood as involving the wrong valence combination: it involves having a positive attitude toward (desiring or aiming at) a base bad.[20] Nonbeneficence does not necessarily involve any similar unfitting attitude. Hence harming or injuring involves a distinctive kind of bad.

I think that this way of understanding nonmaleficence is promising. We should be clear, though, about what it does and what it does not justify. It does, arguably, make harm specially and distinctively bad. But it does not generate a constraint against harming that forbids harming one person to prevent two others being harmed.

Someone might suppose that this therefore cannot be part of a charitable reading of Ross: for Ross is a deontologist, and all deontologists are committed to constraints that forbid harming one to prevent two being harmed. Such an attitude to Ross interpretation strikes me as misconceived and anachronistic. Anyone reading Ross without Anscombe-tinted spectacles should see that Ross is not hostile to consequentialism in the way standard deontologists often are, and is not interested in defending a morality of absolute constraints. Ross's most important innovation is the concept of prima facie duty; he says the basic mistake in ideal utilitarianism is its failure to give proper weight to the highly personal character of duty; he emphasizes the distinction between the general obligation to promote the good and special obligations like that created by a promise. It is surely more charitable to Ross to understand his duty of nonmaleficence in a way that fits into this general framework, rather than reading him as a confused and inexplicit advocate of standard deontology.

7. COMPLETING THE PICTURE: CLASSICAL DEONTOLOGY, OPTIONS, AND COMPARABILITY

I have thus far considered various components of a Rossian normative theory. I argued, following Ross, that the theory should include moral agent-relative intensifiers like those involved in promissory obligation in addition to the pro tanto reason to promote the good. I argued, contra Ross but inspired by Sidgwick, in favor of nonmoral agent-relative intensifiers. And I argued that the theory should not include the constraints or their weakened relatives that are character-istic of standard deontology. It is now time to take stock: to consider both the overall character of the view I am labeling "classical deontology," and the ways in which its components interact.

Start with two comparisons: with Sidgwick and with Kagan. Sidgwick isolates three main "methods of ethics": util-itarianism, egoism, and dogmatic intuitionism (in labeling the normative component of which Broad coined the term "deontology" in its current philosophical sense).[21] And Sidgwick focuses on two conflicts: between utilitarianism and dogmatic intuitionism, and between utilitarianism and egoism. He thinks he can resolve the conflict between utilitarianism and dogmatic intuitionism in favor of utili-tarianism, but that the conflict between utilitarianism and egoism is a standoff: the dualism of practical reason.

Utilitarianism, egoism, and dogmatic intuitionism in-volve considerations of the same kind as the pro tanto reason to promote the good, nonmoral agent-relative intensifiers, and moral agent-relative intensifiers respectively. To get from Sidgwick to classical deontology takes two key intel-lectual moves. The first is to introduce the concept of some-thing contributory: a prima facie duty or a normative reason. Then both conflicts Sidgwick finds between methods can be-come less stark. In particular, the idea that there is an unre-solvable conflict between utilitarianism and egoism can be replaced by the idea that there are both agent-neutral and agent-relative reasons. The second key intellectual move is to draw on Ross's account of special obligations: to see that deontological reasons can be understood as structurally analogous to egoistic agent-relative reasons: as also involving agent-relative intensifiers rather than as the kind of absolute constraints Sidgwick envisages.

Then consider Kagan again. As we saw, Kagan's target is the moderate. The moderate accepts that there is a pro tanto reason to promote the good. But the moderate thinks this reason is limited in two ways: by deontological constraints and by agent-centered options. Kagan aims to argue against both and thus in favor of the extremist position according to which all that remains is the pro tanto reason to promote the good. To advocate classical deontology is to think, as I argued previously, that though constraints are problematic and should be rejected, Rossian special obligations are not similarly problematic and should be accepted.

But we should now further consider the idea of agent-centered options. There may be something right in the idea. To see this, contrast cases in which the pro tanto reason to promote the good competes with promissory obligations with cases in which the pro tanto reason to promote the good competes with nonmoral agent-relative reasons. In the first kind of case, if Ross is right, promissory obligations have significant weight, so it is one's duty to keep a promise in many instances in which breaking the promise would produce a greater amount of overall good. Once the gain in the amount of overall good is great enough, however, the promissory obligation is outweighed. No doubt it is difficult to specify in general terms exactly where this point is; and no doubt there will be some difficult borderline cases. But, on Ross's view, the range of cases where there is something close to a standoff between promissory obligation and the pro tanto reason to promote the good will be quite narrow.

By contrast, the range of cases where there is something close to a standoff between the pro tanto reason to promote the good and nonmoral agent-relative reasons may be very wide. Parfit writes,

> Our partial and impartial reasons are, I believe, only *very imprecisely* comparable. . . . To illustrate . . . we can suppose that in
>
>> *Case One*, I could either save myself from some injury, or act in a way that would save some stranger's life in a distant land,
>
> And that in
>
>> *Case Two*, I could save either my own life or the lives of several distant strangers.
>
> In both cases . . . I would . . . be *rationally* permitted, I believe, to act in either way. In *Case One* I would have sufficient reasons either to save myself from some injury or to save this stranger's life. And I might have such reasons whether my injury would be as little as losing one finger, or as great as losing both legs. In *Case Two*, I would have sufficient reasons to save either my own life or the lives of several strangers. And I might have such reasons whether the number of these strangers would be two or two thousand. Though my reason to save *two* strangers would be *much* weaker than my reason to save *two thousand* strangers, both these reasons might be neither weaker nor stronger than my reason to save my own life. If these claims are true, the relative strength of these two kinds of reason is very imprecise. (OWM 1, 137–38)

If Parfit is basically right here, as I think he is, then there is an important difference between nonmoral agent relative reasons on the one side and the pro tanto reason to promote the good and special obligations on the other. The pro tanto reason to promote the good and special obligations are (to use Parfit's terminology) fairly precisely comparable. By contrast, either of these kinds of reasons is only very imprecisely comparable with nonmoral agent-relative reasons. These facts can be expressed or framed (as I just did, following Parfit) in terms of comparability. But there are other ways of framing or expressing them. One alternative would be to think in terms of options; another, following Joshua Gert, would be to think in terms of a contrast between justifying and requiring reasons.[22] There are interesting questions as to which of these ways of framing the facts involved is to be preferred. But in articulating classical deontology there is no need, I think, to take a firm stand on these questions. So long as we recognize that there is a contrast, that cases where special obligations compete against the pro tanto reason to promote the good look importantly different from cases where either of those compete against nonmoral agent-relative reasons, we can remain neutral as to the best way to frame that contrast.

8. CLASSICAL DEONTOLOGY VERSUS AUDI'S VALUE-BASED INTUITIONISM

The two contemporary philosophers who have done the most to systematically develop normative views inspired by reflection on Ross are Robert Audi and Jonathan Dancy. In significant ways Audi's project is very like mine here—a project of philosophical interpretation of Rossian intuitionism, of giving the most plausible contemporary version of Ross's ideas. Thus, for instance, Audi says chapter 2 of *The Good*

in the Right[23] sets forth a position that constitutes a broadly
Rossian intuitionism, but is developed further than Ross's
view, in part by extension in some places, in part by rectifying
some errors (3). But Audi ends up with a philosophical interpretation very different from mine. Audi argues for what he
calls "value-based intuitionism," a blending of Rossian and
Kantian ideas. On Audi's view,

> Rossian principles of duty can be clarified, rationalized, and
> to some extent unified both by values and by wider moral
> principles. (141)

The wider moral principles to which Audi appeals are versions
of Kant's categorical imperative (specifically the universal
law and end-in-itself formulae). The kind of grounding in
values he proposes is what he calls "ontic grounding," which
he defines as follows:

> To say that a (moral) principle is (at least in part) *ontically
> grounded* in a value is roughly to say that it is *true* at least in
> part because action in accord with the principle is at least a
> partial realization of the value. (141)

There are here familiar Kantian ideas that are part of the
standard anticonsequentialist repertoire in contemporary
moral philosophy: values as attaching to persons rather than
to states of affairs; values as requiring respect rather than
promotion; a unification in terms of requirements to treat
people as ends and not as means.

When Audi comes to list the prima facie duties which
are central to a value-based Kantianism, in chapter 5, it is
striking that what he adds to Ross all brings Ross closer to
twenty-first-century deontologists and Kantians. Thus he

adds a prohibition on injury as well as harm; an independent duty of veracity (whereas Ross derived the duty of veracity from the duty of fidelity); a duty of justice that is unlike Ross's in that it cannot be treated as simply a requirement to promote a higher-order good; an asymmetric duty to enhance and preserve freedom; and a duty of respect.

Deciding which is the better reading of Ross involves us in interrelated issues of textual interpretation and philosophical plausibility. As to textual interpretation, classical deontology is much closer to what Ross actually says than is Audi's value-based intuitionism. To get classical deontology we simply begin with ideal utilitarianism, then spell out what is involved in Ross's famous claim that ideal utilitarianism ignores or does not do full justice to the highly personal character of duty. We spell it out by attending to what Ross says about the nonutilitarian duty he treats most fully, the duty to keep promises. What we end up with fits with what he says in a number of places in summarizing his view, for instance on page 319 in the *Foundations*:

> There are several branches of duty which apparently cannot be grounded on productivity of the greatest good. There appears to be a duty . . . of fulfilling promises, a duty of making compensation . . . a duty of rendering a return for services we have received, and these cannot be explained as forms of the duty of producing the greatest good.

It is true that the duty of nonmaleficence raises a complication—though one which I have argued can be addressed. But even if my treatment of nonmaleficence in section 5 does not work, and so interpreting Ross as a classical deontologist requires removing nonmaleficence from the list of prima facie duties, we still have a list a good deal closer to Ross's than the list Audi gives in chapter 5 of *The Good in the Right*.

Classical deontology differs from consequentialism by adding something distinctively agent-relative, which (unlike absolute prohibitions) I have argued is in principle neither puzzling nor problematic. Audi, instructively, seems to want to go the other way: when he encounters something that seems agent-relative, he wants to explain it away in terms of deontic requirements. Thus he writes,

> It is certainly not obvious that the force of agent-relative reasons is not derivative from one's contribution to intrinsic value *together with* deontic considerations that are also organically conceived. If it is, the point would be explicable by the value-based Kantian intuitionism I have presented. (155)

I regard this as the wrong way around. I have argued that deontological reasons conceived as constraints or prohibitions are problematic while agent-relative reasons are not. So it is much better to explain the deontological in terms of the agent-relative than vice versa.

As to unification, classical deontology seems to me much closer to the spirit of Ross than value-based intuitionism does. As Hurka points out,[24] Ross himself was quite skeptical of the coherence of the humanity formula, and not at all inclined to appeal to it to unify the apparently disparate prima facie duties. By contrast, what classical deontology implies about unity is really very Rossian in character. Classical deontology says that, just as there are a small number of distinct goods, there are a small number of distinct agent-relative intensifiers. Neither list can be more fully unified than that.

"Loyalty to the facts is worth more than a symmetrical architectonic or a hastily reached simplicity" (RG 23).

As I have been emphasizing, classical deontology makes Ross much closer to consequentialism, and much further from Kant, than Audi wants Ross to be. This strikes me as an interpretive advantage. It is anachronistic in reading Ross (or Broad) to assume that he harbored the kind of hostility to consequentialism characteristic of Anscombe, of Kant, and of some contemporary Kantians. Ross treats Moore with great respect. He thinks Moore is mistaken about the normative; but he doesn't think he is corrupt or crazy, he thinks rather that he is in important ways close to the truth. Broad, who as we saw arrived independently at a view strikingly like Ross's, famously thought Sidgwick's *Methods* "on the whole the best treatise on moral theory that has ever been written" (*Five Types*, 143). It would thus be a mistake to assume that the fact that Audi's interpretation creates a greater distance between Ross and traditional consequentialism than mine does counts in favor of Audi's interpretation. Rather, the closer relationship between classical deontology and traditional consequentialism seems to me an interpretive advantage of classical deontology over Audi's value-based intuitionism.

9. CLASSICAL DEONTOLOGY AND PARTICULARISM

Like Audi, Jonathan Dancy is inspired by and aims to improve on Ross. Unlike Audi, he would not claim that the position he arrives at is Rossian; so the question for this section is not how best to interpret Ross, but how to locate and defend classical deontology in the light of Dancy's arguments for particularism. And Dancy's work in another way contrasts with Audi's: while Audi argues for more theoretical unity than is, or I have argued should be, found in Ross, Dancy is famous for arguing for much less. In *Ethics without Principles*[25] one central thesis he defends is holism, according to which

> A feature that is a reason in one case may be no reason at all, or an opposite reason, in another. (73)

In arguing for holism, Dancy gives lots of examples of features that are reason-giving only contingently and in particular contexts: that there will be lots of people there, or that there seems to me to be something red there. These features could very easily switch valence or be normatively irrelevant. The Rossian shares with many other moral theorists the idea that not all reason-giving features are like this. To use J. O. Urmson's terminology, Ross thinks there are some "primary reasons."[26] Consider the fact that an action will cause someone to feel pain. Of it, at least the following seems true: absent further contextual specification, the fact that an action will cause someone pain counts against doing it.

The philosophers I know of whose view is closest to classical deontology are David McNaughton and Piers Rawling (unlike me, they do not defend their view *as an interpretation of Ross*). They argue against Dancy's earlier articulations of particularism in "Unprincipled Ethics"; Dancy replies in *Ethics without Principles*, particularly chapter 7; and McNaughton and Rawling respond in "Contours of the Practical Landscape."[27] I will draw on this exchange both to make the case against Dancy and in favor of Rossian primary reasons, and to explore McNaughton and Rawling's own position.

In "Unprincipled Ethics," McNaughton and Rawling begin with a Rossian view according to which there are "weak" moral principles. Their main example is a principle of justice.

> The fact that an act would be just is always a reason in favour of doing it . . . justice is a *universally right-making* feature of acts. (257)

Dancy denies that there are any correct such principles. Inspired by McDowell, McNaughton and Rawling claim that there are, but that all such principles are like the principle of justice in that they involve thick moral concepts. There are, that is, no true principles which give *nonmoral* features invariant valence.

Dancy responds at the start of chapter 7 of *Ethics without Principles*. He allows that justice may be a universally right-making feature, but denies that anything else on Ross's list of prima facie duties is. And he suggests that even justice is not an invariant reason but only a "default reason." As he explains,

> a default reason is a consideration that is reason-giving unless something prevents its being so. . . . Some features may be set up to be reasons, in advance as it were, although it is always possible for them on occasions to fail to give us the reasons they are set up to give. (112)

McNaughton and Rawling respond in "Contours of the Moral Landscape." They do so in part by defending the claim that there are invariant reasons rather than merely default reasons: the fact that your act would cause someone else undeserved harm counts against in all circumstances. They raise objections to the concept of a default reason. And they develop their own view more fully than in the earlier paper in two important ways. First they provide an inventory of the kinds of reasons there are:

> We see reasons as falling into three and only three categories—the personal, the special, and those associated with considerations of value. Roughly, "personal reasons" are reasons you have to benefit yourself; "special reasons" are reasons to benefit those to whom you stand in special relationships of various sorts; and "value reasons" are reasons you have to promote the general good. (252)

And, second, they lay out a framework for conceptualizing and weighing reasons. The framework involves a key distinction between welfare or benefit (goodness to or for an agent) and value (goodness simpliciter). With this distinction on board, they endorse an additive approach to weighing reasons according to which

> Once one has assessed the separate weight of each element, evaluative judgment consists of adding up the pros and cons to see which side is weightier. (260)

Unsurprisingly, I think McNaughton and Rawling are much closer to the truth on these issues than Dancy. But in some important ways I would not defend a Rossian position in just the way McNaughton and Rawling do. Consider in turn three issues raised in the course of their exchange with Dancy.

First, there is the question of the character of Ross's principles of prima facie duty. Should they be understood, as

McNaughton and Rawling propose, as specifying invariant reasons; or is it enough, as Dancy suggests, to see them as specifying default reasons?

Contra McNaughton and Rawling, I think it would be perfectly acceptable to regard Ross's principles as specifying (merely) default reasons. For, as Dancy explicitly notes, default reasons are fully explanatorily adequate:

> One could say that if a default reason-giving feature does give
> us a reason in [a] context, there is nothing to explain. (113)

McNaughton and Rawling object in part that default reasons so understood are incompatible with other aspects of Dancy's view, which may be true but is not relevant to our question here. But they object also to the notion of explanation involved in the concept of a default reason: that (problematically) what is needed is a non-enquirer-relative account of explanation. I think this objection fails. For invariant reasons share with default reasons the key feature of being fully explanatorily adequate, of properly ending chains of justification. So one cannot argue for invariant reasons and against default reasons on the grounds that the needed notion of explanatory adequacy is unavailable; it has to be available to make sense of invariant reasons just as much as to make sense of default reasons.

Dancy allows that Ross may have succeeded in specifying default reasons, but not (with the possible exception of justice) invariant reasons:

> I would have thought it obvious that one does not always
> have even a prima facie duty to do what one has promised
> to do, and the same goes for making reparation for harm. . . .
> It may of course be that fidelity and gratitude are default

reasons—a possibility that might give [McNaughton and Rawling] ... much of what they want. (120–21)

I am more inclined than McNaughton and Rawling just to accept Dancy's concession and not insist that Rossian principles specify invariant reasons.

Second, there is the question whether the relevant Rossian principles all involve thick moral concepts. Here McNaughton and Rawling's picture differs strikingly from the picture in Broad, who suggests that

> Moral characteristics are always dependent upon certain other characteristics which can be described in purely neutral non-moral terms. Call those non-moral characteristics whose presence in anything confers rightness or wrongness on it *right-tending* and *wrong-tending* characteristics.[28]

If we accept for the sake of argument the correctness of Ross's list of right-tending and wrong-tending characteristics, the key question is whether those characteristics "can be described in purely neutral, non-moral terms." I take it that if the terms used to describe the characteristics do not need to be defined in terms of good, ought, right, or reason, then Broad is right; whereas if the terms used to describe the characteristics themselves have to be defined in terms of good, ought, right, or reason, then McNaughton and Rawling are right.

We have been suggesting that Ross's right-tending and wrong-tending characteristics fall into two distinct categories. One category is productivity of goods. It is a right-tending characteristic of (or reason to do) something that it will produce virtue, or produce knowledge, or produce pleasure. The other category is the category of special reasons or agent-relative intensifiers: it is an extra reason to do something that it will produce a good for someone to whom one made a promise, or previously harmed, or received previous benefit from.

McNaughton and Rawling suggest that none of the characteristics on this list can be defined in neutral, nonmoral terms. Broad suggests that they can all be so defined. It seems to me that the truth lies somewhere in between.

For, first, it seems to me that there is at least one characteristic on the list, productivity of virtue, which is a very strong candidate to be a moral concept: for a virtue is a trait it is good to have (or something similar). Now someone committed to defending Broad's position could try saying that we see (e.g.) that productivity of any specific virtue (courage, say) is a right-tending characteristic, that courage (unlike virtue in general) can be nonmorally defined, and that we see productivity of courage as reason-giving without having to think of courage under the guise of a virtue. But I think this is a stretch. And, as McNaughton and Rawling's emphasis on justice particularly in the earlier paper suggests, what is true of virtue for Ross is also true of justice; for, for Ross, justice is a higher-order good involving the proportioning of happiness to virtue, so if virtue is a moral concept in Ross, then so is justice.

On the other hand, it seems to me at least equally plausible that some characteristics on the list are nonmoral. Two examples are productivity of pain and promising. It seems to me very plausible that pain can be nonmorally defined, and that the fact that an action will produce pain is at least a default reason against it. And it does not seem to me that the thought of productivity of pain as a reason-giving feature needs to be mediated by the independent thought of pain as bad. Second, it seems to me that (as work of John Searle's referred to by McNaughton and Rawling suggests)[29] the notion of a promise can be nonmorally defined, but that the fact that I promised to do X is at least a default reason in favor of doing X.

McNaughton and Rawling in effect argue against the latter example in their earlier paper. They point out that to have moral weight, promises have to meet various conditions, including not being made under duress and not being promises to do something immoral. Since (some of) these conditions cannot be described in purely nonmoral terms, promising is in the relevant sense a moral concept. I am unpersuaded by this argument. Following Dancy, I am inclined to treat these conditions as defeaters. And once we do so, I think we see that McNaughton and Rawling's argument is unpersuasive. What they need to show is that all favorers or intensifiers have to be described in moral terms; and this conclusion is not established by showing that (some of) their defeaters have to be described in moral terms. The same point applies to the example of pain, where it may be clearer. Suppose, as Ross thinks, that the negative reason-giving force of the fact that an action will cause pain is canceled if the pain is deserved. This surely would not be sufficient to establish that "causing pain" is a moral characteristic; that the reason-giving force of a characteristic has some defeater that has to be described in moral terms does not show that the characteristic itself has to be described in moral terms.

Third, there is the question how to frame the Rossian view, and whether to endorse the idea that evaluative judgment is essentially (merely) additive. The inventory of types of reason that McNaughton and Rawling gives is very much in line with classical deontology as we have been developing it. But there is a difference in the rudimentary mathematical models we employ. Following Ross (and drawing on Dancy), I have been emphasizing a distinction between favorers and agent-relative intensifiers. This goes with a basic model that is not merely additive (even before one introduces further possibilities like defeaters). By contrast, McNaughton and Rawling treat all reasons as favorers by relying on their distinction between value and benefit.

I do not think the difference here is very significant. Very likely the two alternatives are just notational variants. But I do see some reasons to prefer my model. McNaughton and Rawling's concept of benefit seems to me less intuitively satisfactory than the concept of an agent-relative intensifier. Consider the case of promising. In the ordinary sense of 'benefit,' as I would see it, what is promised is a benefit to the promisee. But the further key point is that the *weight* of this benefit *in the deliberations of the promiser* is greater because of the promise. McNaughton and Rawling need to describe both these facts using their technical notion of a benefit; my sense is that the facts can be described a good deal more straightforwardly using the language of favorers and intensifiers.

More generally, I suspect that I differ from McNaughton and Rawling in my attitude to the set of distinctions in the theory of reasons that Dancy introduces. In distinguishing between favorers, enablers, and intensifiers (and correspondingly disfavorers, disablers, and attenuators), Dancy moves beyond a simple additive model.[30] Since Dancy himself ends up as a holist and a particularist, one might think that it is dangerous for a Rossian committed to primary reasons to embrace the set of distinctions. I suspect that that perceived danger is one reason McNaughton and Rawling stick to a simple additive model.

I however don't think that it is dangerous for the Rossian to accept Dancy's distinctions. My own view is that the distinctions don't help the case for particularism: they actually help the generalist by allowing for a more nuanced and plausible account of the nature of principles and primary reasons. And indeed I think that Ross himself already in effect embraces Dancy's distinctions (though he does not, of course, use Dancy's terminology). To see that this is so, note first that, as I argued above, Ross in effect treats promises as intensifiers rather than favorers. Then, second, note that in his treatment of the value of pleasure in *The Right and the Good*, Ross in effect introduces disablers:

> A state of pleasure has the property, not necessarily of being good, but of being something that is good if the state has no other characteristic that prevents it from being good. The two characteristics that may interfere with its being good are (a) that of being contrary to desert, and (b) that of being a state which is the realization of a bad disposition. (RG 138)

Note, third and finally, that Ross also moves away from a simple additive model in embracing Moore's principle of organic unities (though he isn't persuaded by most of Moore's examples) (RG 68–73). The Rossian, it seems to me, should here follow Ross himself: embrace Dancy's distinctions but reject his particularism.

I have thus far often ignored or anyway not highlighted the distinction between monistic utilitarianism and pluralistic ideal utilitarianism. My excuse is that I will focus on this distinction in chapter 4, and endorse a modified version of Ross's argument for moderate pluralism against hedonism. I should end this chapter by being fully explicit about the proposed catalog of intrinsically reason-giving features

with which we will then end up. Taking just the key positive
features (the favorers and intensifiers, not the corresponding
disfavorers and attenuators), the provisional Rossian list
(amended, as I argued earlier in this chapter to eliminate
any basic role for the harm/benefit asymmetry, and, as I will
argue in the next chapter, to make pleasure and pain straightforwardly intrinsically good) goes as follows:

> *Intrinsic favorers.* The fact that an action will produce pleasure;
> the fact that an action will produce virtue; the fact that an ac-
> tion will produce knowledge; the fact that an action will pro-
> duce justice.
>
> *Intrinsic agent-relative intensifiers of reasons to produce goods.*
> The fact that I promised to produce that good; the fact that
> I harmed a person in the past; the fact that a person benefited
> me in the past; the fact that a pain or pleasure is mine rather
> than someone else's.

NOTES

1. Thomas Hurka, *British Ethical Theorists from Sidgwick to Ewing*
   (Oxford: Oxford University Press, 2014), 182–83.
2. See Robert Audi, *The Good in the Right* (Princeton: Princeton
   University Press, 2004). Further page references will be placed
   in the text.
3. See David McNaughton and Piers Rawling, "Contours of the
   Practical Landscape," in David Bakhurst, Brad Hooker, and
   Margaret Olivia Little, eds., *Thinking about Reasons: Themes
   from the Philosophy of Jonathan Dancy* (Oxford: Oxford
   University Press, 2013), esp. 252–59. See also their "Agent-
   Relativity and the Doing-Happening Distinction," *Philosophical
   Studies* 63.2 (1991): 167–85. Though inspired by Ross, unlike
   me they do not develop and argue for their view as an *interpre-
   tation* of Ross.

4. C. D. Broad, *Ethics*, ed. C. Lewy (Dordrecht: Martinus Nijhoff, 1985), 197–98.
5. Shelly Kagan, *The Limits of Morality* (Oxford: Clarendon Press, 1989). Further page references will be placed in the text.
6. See Robert Shaver, "Sidgwick's Axioms and Consequentialism," *Philosophical Review* 123.2 (April 2014): 173–204.
7. Pickard-Cambridge criticized Ross in a series of three articles: W. A. Pickard-Cambridge, "Two Problems About Duty (I.)," *Mind 41*.161 (1932): 72–96; "Two Problems about Duty (II.)," *Mind 41*.162 (1932): 145–72; "Two Problems about Duty (III.)," *Mind 41*.163 (1932): 311–40. For a nice treatment of Ross and Pickard-Cambridge, see Anthony Skelton's *Stanford Encyclopedia of Philosophy* article on Ross, section 4.1.
8. In *Ethics* Broad introduces a different term—distributive obligations—to label what I am here calling "agent-relative intensifiers." He writes,

> It is worthwhile to notice that a very important subdivision of ostensibly non-teleological obligations is connected with limitations on teleological obligation. These may be called *distributive obligations*. It is commonly held, e.g., that a person is under a more urgent obligation to do good and to prevent harm to his parents or his children than to strangers. (*Ethics*, 151–52)

9. T. M. Scanlon, *What We Owe to Each Other* (Cambridge, MA: Harvard University Press, 1998), 296.
10. I think the agent-relative intensifier interpretation is the best charitable interpretation of this critical passage in Sidgwick. I don't claim that it is the only possible interpretation or the most textually straightforward interpretation. For more on this see my *Sidgwickian Ethics* (New York: Oxford University Press, 2011), chapter 5, especially 127–31. I don't there employ the term "agent-relative intensifier," but what I say can readily be reframed using it.
11. Roger Crisp, "The Dualism of Practical Reason," *Proceedings of the Aristotelian Society* 96 (1996): 61.
12. Roger Crisp, *Reasons and the Good* (Oxford: Oxford University Press, 2006), 133.

110 | ROSSIAN ETHICS

13. C. D. Broad, "Self and Others," in David Cheney, ed., *Broad's Critical Essays in Moral Philosophy* (London: George Allen and Unwin, 1971), 280.
14. Broad, "Self and Others," 266.
15. The framework of the debate between Moore and Ross (and other contemporaries) is largely similar to the framework of the debate in later work like Kagan's *The Limits of Morality* and Scheffler's *The Rejection of Consequentialism*. We start by assuming that there are agent-neutral consequentialist reasons. The question then is whether we should also admit further reasons (special obligations in Ross, options and constraints in Scheffler and Kagan). I am here accepting this framework, and arguing that Ross (mixed with some Sidgwick) gives us an attractive theory, adding to agent-neutral consequentialism something in the ballpark of options but nothing in the ballpark of constraints.

In recent years a sophisticated literature has developed focused on the possibility of "consequentializing" supposedly nonconsequentialist moral and normative theories. Important work in this literature includes Jamie Dreier, "In Defense of Consequentializing," in Mark Timmons, ed., *Oxford Studies in Normative Ethics*, vol. 1 (New York: Oxford University Press, 2011), 97–119; Douglas Portmore, "Consequentializing Moral Theories," *Pacific Philosophical Quarterly* 88 (2007): 39–73, and *Commonsense Consequentialism* (New York: Oxford University Press, 2011), especially chapter 4; and Campbell Brown, "Consequentialize This!" *Ethics* 121.4 (2011): 739–71. A key claim in this literature is what Portmore calls "the deontic equivalence thesis" and Dreier "the extensional equivalence thesis": that all plausible moral theories can be represented as forms of consequentialism.

The question arises whether the deontic equivalence thesis undermines the rationale for the framework within which I am working. Someone might say: given the deontic equivalence thesis, there is no good justification for two crucial ideas: (1) the idea that we should begin with a traditional consequentialist theory and (2) the idea that constraints are especially problematic.

One kind of response is that (1) and (2) are defensible even if the deontic equivalence thesis is true. Suppose that we cannot defend (1) by claiming that traditional consequentialist reasons are (uniquely) acceptable because any theory that rejects them is incompatible with consequentialism. And suppose that we cannot defend (2) by claiming that constraints are especially problematic because they are incompatible with consequentialism. It is still possible to defend (1) and (2) in alternate ways.

Such alternate defenses of (1) and (2) could in principle take various forms. The form I like draws on Nagel's *The View from Nowhere*. In defending (1), I would urge that the most compelling reasons there are are agent-neutral consequentialist reasons, specifically agent-neutral consequentialist reasons to reduce pain and increase pleasure. Put another way, if you want to convince a reasons-skeptic that there are reasons, start with these. Nagel says, inter alia, "I am not an ethical hedonist, but I think pleasure and pain are very important . . . [and] sensory pleasure is good and pain bad, no matter whose they are" (156). In defending (2), I would claim that deontological constraints are "formally puzzling" in the kind of way Nagel articulates on page 178: "We can understand how autonomous agent-relative reasons might derive from the specific projects and concerns of the agent, and we can understand how neutral reasons might drive from the interests of others, giving each of us reason to take them into account. But how can there be relative reasons to respect the claims of others?"

I don't think these defenses of (1) and (2) depend on rejecting or ignoring the implications of the deontic equivalence thesis. I thus think it can make sense to start where Ross starts and proceed as Ross proceeds even if the deontic equivalence thesis is true.

Another possibility is to deny that consequentialized theories in general share the appeal and advantages of traditional consequentialism. Interestingly, this is the line Ross himself takes when he considers something close to consequentializing in Lecture V of the *Foundations*. He says:

Mr. Katkov denies the possibility of any *prima facie* obligation which can conflict with the duty of producing the best state of affairs, on the general ground that 'better' simply means that which it is right to prefer. This is simply a cutting of the knot. The position is this. Those who think as I do, think . . . that there is a *prima facie* duty to fulfil promises even when no greater good can be foreseen as likely to come into being by the promise being kept than by its being broken; and we think that this shows that the rule "produce the greatest good" is not the only rule of conduct. The followers of Brentano agree with us in thinking that when we have made a promise we are under a special obligation to the promise, but differ from us in thinking that it can be brought under the general rule "choose the greatest good." But instead of trying to point out wherein the specific good to be produced by keeping promises consists, they content themselves with saying "it must be the greatest good because it is what we ought to produce." The utilitarian says "you ought to do so-and-so because by doing so you will produce the greatest possible good": the follower of Brentano says "do what you ought to do, and you may be sure that in doing so you will be choosing the greatest good, since 'better' means nothing but that to prefer which is right."

Mr. Katkov sees that if this all that 'better' means, his principle "you ought to choose the best of what is attainable" is in danger of being a mere tautology. . . . Unless we can see a goodness in the state of affairs produced by a fulfilment of a promise—a goodness not resting on or consisting in the fact that we ought to fulfil the promise— we cannot say that the duty of fulfilling the promise rests on the general duty of producing what is good. (F 107–8)

Ross here in effect denies that the consequentializer manages to locate and preserve the key appealing feature of traditional consequentialism. Ross thinks that traditional consequentialism is appealing only when it relies on a prior and independent conception of what makes states of affairs good to justify the claim that you ought to produce the greatest possible good. This appeal is not preserved if the good is simply defined in terms of whatever you ought to produce. Mark Schroeder develops an argument of this kind in "Teleology, Agent-Relative Value, and 'Good,'" *Ethics* 117 (2007): 265–95.

16. Thomas Nagel, *The View from Nowhere* (Oxford: Oxford University Press, 1986). Page references will be placed in the text.

17. An important anthology on the topic is Bonnie Steinbock and Alastair Norcross, eds., *Killing and Letting Die* (New York: Fordham University Press, 1994). Frances Kamm has done particularly noteworthy recent work articulating and defending a deontological view. See, for example, her *Intricate Ethics* (Oxford: Oxford University Press, 2008). For a brief presentation of a consequentialist view see Peter Singer, *Practical Ethics*, 3rd ed. (Cambridge: Cambridge University Press, 2011), 178–86.

18. In note 2 on page 85 of *The Rejection of Consequentialism*, Scheffler briefly notices the possibility of the kind of deontology I attribute to Ross. He says, *inter alia*

> I will not directly discuss any specific proposals that might be made for motivating *only* those agent-centered restrictions which prohibit the breaking of one's promises or the neglect of one's special obligations. And, strictly speaking, this leaves it open to a defender of a fully agent-centered outlook to maintain that those restrictions have a rationale of the appropriate form which is independent of any putative rationale for restrictions like [the restriction against harming some undeserving person], and which remains compelling even if doubt is cast on the strength of supposed general rationales for agent-centered restrictions, and on the strength of specific rationales for agent-centered restrictions against harming in particular.

19. For a fuller discussion of such recursive principles, see Hurka, *Virtue, Vice, and Value* (Oxford: Oxford University Press, 2003). For a briefer discussion of their role in the Sidgwick-to-Ewing

school, see Hurka, *British Ethical Theorists*, chapter 10, especially 217–18. I discuss these recursive principles in connection with Ross's account of virtue in chapter 4, section 4.
20. A neutral attitude to a base bad would also be unfitting.
21. For the introduction, see *Five Types*, 206–7. For discussion, see Robert Louden, "Towards a Genealogy of 'Deontology,'" *Journal of the History of Philosophy* 34.4 (1996): 571–92 and Jens Timmerman, "What's Wrong with 'Deontology'?," *Proceedings of the Aristotelian Society* 115 (2015): 75–92.
22. See, inter alia, Joshua Gert, "Requiring and Justifying: Two Dimensions of Normative Strength," *Erkenntnis* 59 (2003): 5–36.
23. Robert Audi, *The Good in The Right* (Princeton: Princeton University Press, 2004), 3. Further page references will be placed in the text.
24. Thomas Hurka, "Audi's Marriage of Ross and Kant."
25. Dancy, *Ethics without Principles*. Page references will be placed in the text.
26. J. O. Urmson, "A Defense of Intuitionism," *Proceedings of the Aristotelian Society* 75 (1975): 111–19.
27. David McNaughton and Piers Rawling, "Unprincipled Ethics," in Brad Hooker and Margaret Olivia Little, eds., *Moral Particularism* (Oxford: Clarendon Press, 2000), 256–75; McNaughton and Rawling, "Contours of the Practical Landscape." Page references will be placed in the text.
28. C. D. Broad, "Some of the Main Problems of Ethics," in *Broad's Critical Essays*, 228.
29. John Searle, "How to Derive 'Ought' from 'Is,'" *Philosophical Review* 73 (1964): 43–58.
30. See, in particular, *Ethics without Principles*, chapter 3.

4

WHAT THINGS ARE GOOD?

I ARGUED IN THE PREVIOUS chapter for a structurally simple account of reasons intermediate between utilitarianism and absolutist deontology. There are (as utilitarianism says) goods, and reasons to promote them; but there are also (contrary to utilitarianism) a small number of agent-relative intensifiers.

In a different but related way, the moderate pluralism about the good Ross presents in chapter 5 of *The Right and the Good* can be seen as a structurally simple accommodation of the most important utilitarian and antiutilitarian claims about the good. As Ross summarizes this moderate pluralism

> Four things . . . seem to be intrinsically good—virtue, pleasure, the allocation of pleasure to the virtuous, and knowledge. (RG 141)

If we set aside knowledge, the list comprises three items: the thing that utilitarians claim is only intrinsic good (pleasure); the thing that Kant claims is the only thing with intrinsic moral worth (virtue), and the morally significant relation between the two (desert). If we take perfection to have two forms, moral and intellectual, its three basic goods (virtue, knowledge, and happiness) are also just those Sidgwick points to when he remarks close to the start of the *Methods*,

> *Prima facie* the only two ends which have a strongly and widely supported claim to be regarded as rational ultimate ends are . . . Happiness and Perfection. (ME 9)

Ross's moderate pluralism about the good is less original than his moderate pluralism about the right. His introduction of the concept of prima facie duty, our subject in chapter 2, was a fundamental innovation in moral theory. And his articulation of a new form of deontology utilizing the concept of prima facie duty, our subject in chapter 3, was distinctive within the intuitionist tradition, a significant break from predecessors like Sidgwick, Moore, and Rashdall.[1] By contrast, Ross is not distinctive in defending some version of moderate pluralism about the good. That had been done before by Rashdall and by Moore.[2]

Nonetheless, I shall argue in this chapter that there is much to be said for Ross's version. His list of intrinsic goods is a plausible starting list. And much of what he says about virtue (which he discusses at some length) and about the value of knowledge (which he discusses much more briefly) is also plausible.

There is, however, another aspect of Ross's treatment which I shall argue is wholly mistaken: a persistent impulse to downgrade happiness relative to virtue. This radical antihedonism takes two main forms: the claim in *The Right and the Good* that virtue is lexically prior to pleasure and the claim in the *Foundations* that pleasure is not intrinsically good. In rejecting Ross's view about the relative value of happiness and virtue, I will first focus on his defense of these radically antihedonist claims in his treatment of pleasure. I will then turn to his treatment of virtue, and argue that, while his account of virtue is attractive, it is in tension with his radical antihedonism.

1. THE EASY CASE FOR MODERATE PLURALISM

Ross makes (what I will call) the "easy case" for moderate pluralism in the quite brief chapter 5 of *The Right and the Good*. He begins by arguing against the hedonist. He thus at this point provisionally admits that pleasure is good; the question then at issue is whether (as hedonists hold) pleasure is the *only* thing that is good, or whether, as pluralists hold, things other than pleasure are also good. His basic argumentative resource in the chapter is the appeal to a particular kind of intuitions—intuitions about the relative goodness of quite abstractly described possible worlds. It will be useful to have a shorthand label for such intuitions and the arguments that invoke them. I propose to call them "abstract world intuitions" and "abstract world arguments."

Ross first appeals to an abstract world intuition in arguing against hedonism and for the claim that virtue (too) is intrinsically good:

> If anyone is inclined to doubt [that virtue is intrinsically good] ... it seems to me enough to ask the question whether, of two states of the universe holding equal amounts of pleasure, we should really think no better of one in which the actions and dispositions of all the persons were thoroughly virtuous

than of one in which they were highly vicious. To this there can be only one answer. (RG 134)

While the radically antihedonist strand in Ross makes an appearance later in chapter 5, he does also introduce an abstract world intuition to support the claim that pleasure is good:

> Suppose two states of the universe including equal amounts of virtue, but the one including also widespread and intense pleasure and the other widespread and intense pain. (RG 135)

He gives a further abstract world argument to show that the allocation of pleasure to virtue is intrinsically good:

> If we compare two imaginary states of the universe, alike in the total amounts of virtue and vice and of pleasure and pain present in the two, but in one of which the virtuous were all happy and the vicious miserable, while in the other the virtuous were miserable and the vicious happy, very few people would hesitate to say that the first was a much better state of the universe than the second. (RG 138)[3]

And he gives a final abstract world argument for the value of knowledge:

> [Suppose] two states of the universe equal in respect of virtue and of pleasure and of the allocation of pleasure to the virtuous, but such that the persons in the one had a far greater understanding of the nature and laws of the universe than those in the other. Can any one doubt that the first would be a better state of the universe? (RG 139)

Ross's moderate pluralism involves not just the claim that these four things are intrinsically good, but also the claim that nothing else is intrinsically good. I raise the issue of the comprehensiveness of his list at the end of the chapter.

2. ROSS'S PERPLEXITIES ABOUT PLEASURE I: WEIGHING GOODS

In *The Right and the Good* Ross treats pleasure and virtue as good in the same sense. But he argues for a strikingly antihedonist claim about the relative value of pleasure and virtue: the thesis that any amount of virtue (however small) is better than any amount of knowledge (however great), and that any amount of knowledge (however small) is better than any amount of pleasure (however great).[4] Ross's treatment of knowledge raises very interesting issues, some of which I will take up later in this chapter and in chapter 5. But his treatment of the relative value of different goods knowledge is, I think, an additional complication. The core claim for which Ross really wants to argue is that any amount of virtue (however small) is worth more than any amount of pleasure (however great). As he puts it himself,

> *No* amount of pleasure is equal to any amount of virtue . . . virtue belongs to a higher order of value, beginning at a point higher on the scale of value than that which pleasure ever reaches. (RG 150)

Call this claim "the lexical priority of virtue over pleasure."

This claim is immediately problematic: for it appears to be in tension with very plausible abstract world arguments of the sort Ross himself advanced in the previous chapter. As we saw, in arguing provisionally for the intrinsic value of pleasure, Ross invites us to

> Suppose two states of the universe including equal amounts of virtue, but the one including also widespread and intense pleasure and the other widespread and intense pain. (RG 135)

We are clearly supposed to take the first world to be preferable to the second. This conclusion is compatible with Ross's lexical priority claim: for the two worlds he imagines are equal in amounts of virtue, so different amounts of pleasure could serve as tiebreakers even if virtue were lexically prior to pleasure. But now change the thought experiment slightly:

> Suppose two states of the universe including nearly equal amounts of virtue—differing only in that one person on one occasion was less well motivated and acted less well in universe 1 than in universe 2—but such that universe 1 includes also widespread and intense pleasure and universe 2 widespread and intense pain.

It seems to me just as clear that universe 1 is better than and should be chosen over universe 2 in this revised thought experiment as it was that universe 1 should be chosen over universe 2 in Ross's original version of the thought experiment. So there is a very plausible abstract world argument against the lexical priority of virtue over pleasure.

We should then expect that something has gone wrong in Ross's defense of the lexical priority claim; and I shall claim indeed that several things have. He offers three arguments for the claim in *The Right and the Good*. The first argument involves an appeal to the difficulty of finding a precise equivalent in pleasure to some given amount of virtue

> If we take the view [that a certain larger amount of pleasure would more than outweigh a given amount of virtue] . . . we are faced by the question, *what* amount of pleasure is precisely equal in value to a given amount of virtue. . . . And to this question, so long as we think that *some* amount is equal, I see no possibility of an answer or of an approach to one. With regard to pleasure and virtue, it seems to me much more likely to be the truth that *no* amount of pleasure is equal to any amount of virtue. (RG 150)

This argument seems to me unpersuasive. Ross begins the chapter on degrees of goodness by asking about the comparability and commensurability of pleasures. He argues that pleasures are both comparable and commensurable, but that they are only roughly commensurable:

> There seems to be no doubt that in comparing two comparatively simple pleasures, recently experienced, we can sometimes say with the greatest confidence that one was, say, at least twice as intense as the other. We cannot be more precise than this and say that one was just twice, or three times, as intense as the other. That points to the absence of some of the conditions needed for exact commensuration. (RG 143)

If pleasures can be only roughly commensurable so that we cannot say that one was just twice as intense as another, surely pleasure and virtue can also be only roughly commensurable so that we cannot say that some amount of pleasure is precisely equal to some amount of virtue. And the fact that pleasure and virtue are only roughly commensurable then provides no good reason to think that virtue is lexically prior to pleasure, just as the fact that two pleasures are only roughly commensurable provides no good reason to think that one of these pleasures is lexically prior to the other.

The second argument Ross gives plays a more fundamental role in his treatment of the topic in the *Foundations* as well as in *The Right and the Good*:[5]

> The acquisition of pleasure for oneself rarely, if ever, presents itself as a duty, and usually only as something permissible when it does not interfere with duty, while the attainment of moral goodness habitually presents itself as a duty. This surely points to an infinite superiority of virtue over pleasure, a superiority such that no gain in pleasure can make up for a loss in virtue.
>
> But if virtue is better worth aiming at for ourselves than pleasure, it is better worth trying to promote for man in general. (RG 151)

This argument too is problematic. Ross is right that "the acquisition of pleasure for oneself rarely . . . presents itself as a duty." But the question is how to explain this fact: does the best explanation (as Ross suggests here in *The Right and the Good*) support the idea that pleasure is infinitely inferior in value to virtue or (as he later suggests, in the *Foundations*) the idea that pleasure and virtue are not good in the same sense?

I think the best explanation of the fact supports neither conclusion. We can begin with an alternative explanation Ross himself canvasses in the *Foundations*: that, though we do think our own pleasure is good and hence think it is right to produce it, we don't think producing it is a *duty* or an *obligation*. But that is because thinking of producing something as a duty or obligation involves not just the thought that it is right to do it, but also some other distinctive thought.

> It might be said that [getting pleasure or avoiding pain for ourselves] . . . is right, but . . . [not] obligatory, because there is no possibility of a moral conflict, since . . . our natural desire inevitably prompts us to that which it is right for us to do—to seek our own pleasure. I do not think that this suggestion can be accepted; for (1) the act of seeking pleasure for ourselves is not merely not obligatory, but has not even the kind of rightness or fitness which is moral fitness. It seems morally entirely colourless (2) . . . the explanation of its not being felt to be obligatory does not seem to me to meet the case. For it often happens that there is a perfectly natural tendency to seek to give pleasure to some other person, which is just as strong as is in most people the tendency to seek pleasure for themselves. This is noticeably so in maternal love. Yet no one would say that because the mother naturally seeks the happiness of her children she has no duty to seek it. (F 277–78)

We can agree that this alternative explanation as it stands is not fully convincing. But there is a better version of this kind of alternative explanation which Ross himself (as we argued in chapter 2) does not have the conceptual resources to consider. The better explanation involves first distinguishing *moral duties* from *reasons*; then adding a particular specification as to which reasons count as moral duties.

Begin with the distinction between reasons and moral duties. Consider two different possible formulations of the claim that a person's own pain or pleasure is normatively significant:

(1) Each person has a reason to produce pleasure or avoid pain for himself.
(2) Each person has a moral duty to produce pleasure or avoid pain for himself.

It seems to me (1) is much more intuitively plausible than (2). That, I think, is not because our response to (2) involves an intuition about the normative significance of our own pleasures and pains that is more reliable than the intuition involved in our response to (1). It is rather because the term "moral duty" introduces some further distinctively moral thought over and above the thought of our having a reason.

Then add a second idea, different from the one Ross explores in the passage above, as to the nature of this distinctively moral thought: that "moral" and "selfish" are contraries: that if a reason is selfish it is not a moral reason. On this alternative explanation, our own happiness is good, and so there is a reason to produce it. But the reason to produce one's own happiness is a selfish reason. So it is not a moral reason.

This alternative explanation is not available to Ross because, as we saw in chapter 2, he does not distinguish moral duties from reasons. But it meshes in other ways with his thinking, in that some of that thinking seems to involve relatives of the idea that the moral and the selfish are contraries. Specifically, as we will see in section 4, in thinking about the value of different motives he treats the desire for pleasure for oneself as indifferent.[6]

Ross's argument, then, from the claim that we are not conscious of a duty to produce pleasure for ourselves to the conclusion that virtue is infinitely superior to pleasure is quite unconvincing.

Ross offers a third argument for this lexical priority claim in *The Right and the Good*, premised on the existence of bad pleasures:

> It seems clear that when we consider [a pleasure such as the pleasure of cruelty] we are able to say at once that it is bad, that it would have been better that it should not have existed. If the goodness of pleasure were commensurable with the goodness or badness of moral disposition, it would be possible that such a pleasure if sufficiently intense should be good on the whole. But in fact its intensity is a measure of its badness. (RG 151)

This argument too is unconvincing. We can explain the putative facts to which Ross points about bad pleasures without supposing that virtue is lexically superior to pleasure. We need only suppose (as Ross himself elsewhere does) that pleasure is only prima facie good; that its goodness is canceled or that it becomes bad if it is a bad pleasure (RG 136–38). Making that supposition in no way commits us to the view that good or indifferent pleasures are lexically inferior to virtue.

3. ROSS'S PERPLEXITIES ABOUT PLEASURE II: IS PLEASURE INTRINSICALLY GOOD?

In the *Foundations* Ross changed his mind about the lexical priority claim. Unfortunately he adopted instead a position which I shall argue is still less plausible.

One reason Ross changed his mind is that he came to think that a lexical scale is incoherent:

> I now see this . . . to be impossible. If virtue were really on the same scale of goodness as pleasure, then pleasure of a certain intensity, if enjoyed by a sufficiently large number of persons or for a sufficient time, would counterbalance virtue possessed or manifested only by a small number or only for a short time. (F 275)

I think Ross is here mistaken. There is a kind of scale—a lexical scale, unsurprisingly—which would allow any amount of virtue however small to outweigh any amount of pleasure however great. It is true that such a lexical scale is different from the kind of scale Ross has in mind. But a lexical scale is a kind of scale nonetheless. As I argued above, it is very implausible that virtue is lexically superior to pleasure; but that is not because the very idea of a lexical scale is incoherent.

Ross unfortunately was still moved by the two main arguments he earlier took to support the lexical priority of pleasure over virtue—the argument from the fact that there is no duty to produce pleasure for oneself and the argument from the existence of bad pleasures. But, having come to think the lexical priority claim incoherent, he now took the two arguments to support a different conclusion, the conclusion that virtue and pleasure are not good in the same sense. He articulates this new conclusion most fully at two points in Lecture XI of the *Foundations*. First, in introducing the issue about the goodness of pleasure, he writes:

> The first point to which I would draw attention is that, while for the word 'good' when applied to moral dispositions and actions and to intellectual . . . activities we can fairly substitute

'admirable' . . . we cannot do this in the case of pleasant experiences. . . . There is nothing admirable . . . in the mere feeling of pleasure. (F 271)

In later summary, he observes that virtue and knowledge

Are good in a sense which is indefinable, but which may be paraphrased by saying that they are fine or good or admirable activities of the human spirit. . . . Pleasure is never good in this, which I should call the most proper sense of 'good'. But the pleasures of others . . . are good in a secondary sense, viz., that they are morally worthy or suitable objects of satisfaction. Things that are good in the first and most proper sense we have, by a self-evident necessity, a *prima facie* duty to produce. . . . Things that are good in the secondary sense, i.e. the pleasures of others, are also things we have a duty to produce. (F 283)

I shall argue that this revised treatment of goodness is worse than the treatment in *The Right and the Good*. For central aspects of Ross's normative view and of his argumentative strategy require the single fundamental concept of goodness or intrinsic value which he articulates in *The Right and the Good* but rejects in the *Foundations*. Consider first Ross's normative view. As we have seen, he thinks that consequentialism is *part* of the truth, and that its partial truth is one important reason to be interested in goodness. Thus at the start of Lecture IX he observes,

There are two reasons which make it necessary for any student of ethics to devote attention to the nature of goodness. . . . The . . . [second] is that a great part of our duty—indeed, according to a widely accepted theory, the whole of our duty— is to bring what is good into existence. Even if we reject that

theory it must be admitted that where no special duty . . . is
involved, our duty is just to produce as much good as we can.
(F 252)

This view seems to require a single fundamental sense of
goodness or intrinsic value, such that the good is that at
which we ought to aim or that which we ought to produce.
The view is compatible with different claims about whether
goodness in this sense is definable in terms or rightness or is
independent of it: it could be that the good is defined as that
at which we ought to aim; or it could be that the concepts of
intrinsic goodness and rightness are independent and both
irreducible.[7] The idea that consequentialism is part of the
truth fits with either possibility. But it does seem to require
a single concept of intrinsic goodness; and the conceptual
scheme of *The Right and the Good* straightforwardly and ec-
onomically includes this fundamental concept.

By contrast, Ross's proposal in the *Foundations*
introduces unnecessary complexities, because, as he still
endorses the idea that consequentialism is part of the truth,
he still in effect needs the earlier concept of intrinsic goodness. The first unnecessary complexity is that Ross needs it
to be a self-evident truth that we ought to aim at what we
ought to admire. (He says, as we saw above, that this is "a
self-evident necessity.") That is, he needs to connect his new
concept of goodness in the sense of what we ought to admire
to the earlier unitary concept of intrinsic value. The second
complexity is that he needs also to connect goodness in his
second new sense—goodness in the sense of what we ought
to feel satisfaction in—with the earlier concept of intrinsic
value. He needs it to be a further new truth (and, the passage quoted above rather suggests, a further new truth of a

different sort, not exactly self-evident) that we ought to aim at what we ought to feel satisfaction in. A third issue is that, given these further truths, we still need to weigh against one another things that are good in the two different new senses. And, indeed, given that we do, Ross's proposal in the *Foundations* does not obviously succeed in doing the specific job for which he introduced it: why should the fact that virtue and knowledge are good in one sense and pleasure good in another mean that, when we are deciding what we ought to produce or aim at, virtue turns out to be a greater good than pleasure?

The conceptual scheme of *The Right and the Good* also fits much better with an important part of Ross's argumentative strategy—the appeal to abstract world arguments. The question being asked in abstract world arguments is: which world would you *pick* or *choose*? Such arguments, that is, seem to involve appealing to the most generic of positive responses. They do not seem to involve distinguishing different positive responses like admiration and satisfaction.

The main philosophical motivation for Ross's adoption of two different senses of goodness in the *Foundations* seems, as we saw, to be the desire to downgrade pleasure relative to virtue—to provide an alternative to the lexical priority claim advanced in *The Right and the Good*. But it is not the only philosophical motivation. Ross also makes some plausible claims about differences between the ways in which virtue is good and the ways in which pleasure is good. For instance:

> Another way in which the difference between good activities and pleasure is revealed is that, while we can call a man good . . . in respect of his moral actions and dispositions and in respect of his intellectual and artistic activities, any goodness

that pleasure may be supposed to have is not in this way re-
flected on to its enjoyer. A man is not good in respect of the
mere fact of feeling pleasure. (F 271)

There is something right in these claims. But what is right
in them can be perfectly properly accommodated within the
conceptual framework Ross employed in *The Right and the
Good*. Ross there defines the moral good as a subspecies of
the intrinsically good:

> I can best explain what I mean by '*morally* good' by saying that
> it means "good either by being a certain sort of character or by
> being related in one of certain definite ways to a certain sort of
> character". (RG 155)

He thus introduces a distinctive subsidiary class of intrinsically good things of a particular kind. We admire good
character, and admire people who have good characters.
So, we may quite plausibly suggest, moral goodness has a
special relation to admiration that pleasure doesn't have.
But that does not give us any good reason to think that
the most fundamental sense of 'good' is the sense picked
out by 'morally good'. It is much more sensible, rather, as
Ross does in *The Right and the Good*, to regard the morally
good as a subspecies of the intrinsically good, definable in
terms of it.

4. ROSS ON VIRTUE

In both *The Right and the Good* and the *Foundations*,
Ross treats virtue or moral goodness as a matter of the intrinsic value of motives. The argument for this treatment

is most fully developed in the *Foundations*. Ross begins by observing

> What we are apt to think of first, when we ask ourselves what kinds of thing are morally good, is certain types of voluntary action, proceeding from certain motives, such as the wish to do one's duty . . . and we might be disposed therefore to identify moral goodness with goodness of will. But this would be a mistake. For if we hold that actions are morally good when and because they proceed from certain motives, we can hardly fail to ascribe moral goodness to those same desires when they do not lead to action. (F 290)

But, he then argues, even the idea that what is morally good is motives is too restrictive. For, first, we ought to include certain emotions as well as motives; so really what is morally good are interests:

> If desire for another's pleasure is good, so also is satisfaction at his actual pleasure. . . . And if we may group desires and satisfactions together under the heading of 'interests', interests, no less than actions inspired by interests, may be morally good. (F 291)

But even this is still too restrictive. For if felt desires and emotions are morally good, so also is the disposition to have such desires and emotions.

In developing his account of the value of motives, Ross draws particularly on Kant. Ross's view differs in three important ways from Kant's: Ross argues that the motive of duty can properly be treated as an ordinary motive or desire; he argues that though this motive is the best motive it is not the only morally good motive; and he disagrees with what he takes to be Kant's view about the value of actions from mixed motives.[8]

Ross distinguishes and ranks desires or motives in terms of moral goodness. His inventory of motives in *The Right and the Good* is smaller, and yields the following ranking:

(1) The desire to do one's duty
(2) The desire to bring into being something good
(3) The desire to produce some pleasure, or to prevent some pain, for another being
(4) The desire for one's own pleasure
(5) The desire to inflict some pain on another
(6) The desire to bring into being some particular evil
(7) The desire to do what is wrong

Of these, (1), (2), and (3) are of (decreasing) positive value, (4) is indifferent, and (5), (6), and (7) are of (increasing) negative value. Ross thinks (7) is not found among humans, though (5) and (6) are.

The more fine-grained classification scheme in the *Foundations* features eleven desires Ross thinks are actually found among human beings. It is not clear that Ross is committed to a complete ordering of these desires, or at least that he has supplied one. Again we can list the desires in approximate order of moral value, but having done so need to be careful in specifying the order of goodness or badness:

(1) The desire to do one's duty
(2) The desire to do a particular prima facie duty
(3) The generalized desire to promote the moral and intellectual improvement of all human beings

(4) The desire to promote some perfection or good activity in oneself or another

(5) The desire to produce the maximum of pleasure for all individuals

(6) The desire to produce some pleasure for some individual

(7) The desire to produce some pleasure for oneself

(8) The desire to produce the maximum of pleasure for oneself

(9) The desire to produce pain for some individual

(10) The desire to produce the maximum of pain for some individual

(11) The desire to produce moral evil in some other person

Of these, (1) through (6) are of positive value, (7) and (8) are (subject to the proviso noted subsequently) indifferent, and (9) though (11) are of (increasing) negative value. The main thing that makes the scheme in the *Foundations* more fine-grained than the scheme in *The Right and the Good* is the distinction (inspired by Butler's treatment of self-love) between particular and general forms of various desires: thus (1) and (2), (3) and (4), (5) and (6), (8) and (7), and (10) and (9) are pairs where the first is a more general and the second a more specific desire of the same type.[9]

The following complexities mean that Ross is not straightforwardly committed to the ordering of (1) through (11): First, in distinguishing as he does between (1) and (2), (3) and (4), and (5) and (6), Ross clearly thinks the more general motive of a given positive kind better than the less general motive (and he thinks the reverse for motives of a negative kind). But he does not always explicitly consider the relative value of the more general form of a lower motive as against the less general form of the motive above it. He does commit himself to the view that it is better to be motivated by (2), the desire to do a particular prima facie duty, than by (3), the generalized desire to promote the moral and intellectual improvement of all human beings.[10] But we might also ask whether it is better to be motivated by (5), the general desire to produce the maximum of pleasure for all individuals, or by (4), the desire to produce some perfection or good activity in oneself or another. Ross doesn't clearly answer this question. Second, his view about the relative value of (7) and (8) is complex, in that he thinks (8) is always indifferent (of neither positive nor negative value), while specific instances of (7) have positive, zero, or negative value as a function of the value of the particular pleasures that are their objects. Desires for good pleasures have positive value, desires for bad pleasures negative value.

This is Ross's account of the nature of virtue. It seems to me in two ways initially intuitively attractive: Ross argues plausibly (as we saw) for the claim that virtue or moral goodness is a matter of the value of motives. And the position he defends is one that seems an attractive revision of Kant's claims about the value of motives: the motive of duty (as Kant claims) is the highest motive; but other motives, like benevolent ones (contra Kant) are also intrinsically valuable, though less so. As we saw, Ross is also committed to two more general claims about the value of virtue: to the claim that virtue is intrinsically rather than instrumentally valuable; and (in different forms, as we saw, in *The Right and the Good* and in the *Foundations*) to the claim that virtue is vastly more valuable than pleasure. One question to which we will need to return is how well Ross's account of the nature of virtue fits with his account of its value. Is it plausible that virtue, understood as Ross understands it, is intrinsically valuable? And is it plausible that virtue, understood as Ross understands it, has the degree of intrinsic value Ross takes it to have?

To think further about the plausibility of Ross's account of virtue, we can raise a question Ross himself does not really address: is there some unifying explanation of his judgments of the values of different desires? I think that the following is a good initial answer: the desires in question differ in their degree of moral-reasons responsiveness: the more moral-reasons responsive a desire is, the better. This explanation involves two component ideas: that, to be of value, a desire has to be a response to a reason; and that, to be of value, it has to be a response to a *moral* reason. Since (4) in the list from *The Right and the Good* and (7) and (8) from the list in the *Foundations* are *selfish* desires, they are not responses to moral reasons; for "selfish" and "moral" are contraries. (We drew on related ideas earlier.)

The motive of duty, for Ross the highest motive, raises complications. As we saw, Ross himself does not distinguish between reasons and moral reasons (or *reasons* and *prima facie duties*). But, as I argued previously, we should draw this distinction. We can then distinguish the desire to do what there is most reason to do from the desire to do what there is most moral reason to do. And it is natural then to ask: are both of these motives valuable? And, if so, which is the more valuable? Focus for now only on the question whether the motive to do what there is most reason to do is valuable whether or not what there is most reason to do is what there is most moral reason to do. I think that we should provisionally answer yes. The motive to do what there is most reason to do is the motive that most fully responds to the normative considerations; such a full and accurate response is plausibly taken to be intrinsically valuable.

So far we have identified two factors that seem to unify Ross's treatment of the relative value of motives: reasons-responsiveness and unselfishness. We can further distinguish two additional elements that seem, for Ross, to contribute to reasons-responsiveness. First, a desire is more reasons-responsive if it is more *general*: if it is a response to *all* the properties of a particular kind, not just to one of those properties. Second, a desire is more reasons-responsive if it is more *explicit*: if it is a response to a normative property (like goodness) rather than to a normatively significant nonnormative property (like pleasantness). We can then ask of each of the dimensions of desire we have identified—generality, explicitness, unselfishness, and reasons-responsiveness—whether it is plausible that these contribute to the intrinsic value of desires.

Begin with generality. Is Ross right in suggesting, for instance, that the desire to produce the maximum of pleasure for all individuals is more valuable than the desire to produce some pleasure for some individual? If so, why?

Here we need to notice something missing from Ross's lists. Desires, as standardly conceived, have both objects and strengths. In giving his lists Ross does not focus on strengths. But intuitively they matter. It would intuitively be much better to have a strong desire for a great good and a mild desire for a trivial good than to have a strong desire for a trivial good and a mild desire for a great good. Particular desires, conceived simply as such, can be misguided in this way. By contrast, general desires are automatically immune to this kind of misguidedness. In desiring to produce the maximum pleasure of all individuals, one automatically appropriately weighs each individual component pleasure.

Properly to compare the value of particular and general versions of some desire, we should stipulate that the particular desire is not misguided in this way: that it is a particular desire with the right valence and of the right strength. Is Ross's view that the more general desire is more valuable than the particular desire still plausible? It seems to me that it is. The value of a desire is the product of two factors: of the degree to which the desire responds appropriately, in valence and strength to its object; and of the degree of value of the object. General desires (of correct valence and strength) are more valuable than related particular desires (of correct valence and strength) because they are responses to more valuable objects. Generality, then, does seem to matter.

Now consider explicitness. Is it better to be motivated to do some prima facie duty than it is to produce some good? And is it better to be motivated to produce a good than to produce a pleasure?

Some philosophers have famously advocated views potentially contrary in spirit to Ross's: suggesting that (at least sometimes) less explicit motives are better. Bernard Williams famously says that the man who is moved to save his wife rather than a stranger by the thought that in situations of this kind it is permissible to save one's wife has

> one thought too many: it might have been hoped by some (for instance, by his wife) that his motivating thought, fully spelled out, would be the thought that it was his wife.[11]

Williams is clearly not here interested in the *moral* value of motives. But his claim might inspire someone to argue that the less explicit motive has greater intrinsic value, even if that intrinsic value is not moral.

I am inclined to side here neither with Ross nor with (this extrapolation from) Williams. We should, I think, make the same stipulation with respect to more and less explicit motives as we made above with respect to more and less general motives: that each responds appropriately, in valence and strength, to its object. Given this stipulation, I am then inclined to think the motives equally valuable: to think that it does not matter to their value how morally or normatively explicit they are.

Our initial unifying explanation of Ross's judgments about the value of motives identified two unifying factors: degree of reasons-responsiveness and unselfishness. We identified two further factors that, for Ross, seem to contribute to degree of reasons-responsiveness: generality and explicitness. And we argued that though generality does make motives better, explicitness does not. Properly conceived, reasons-responsiveness seems to be a product of two factors: the appropriateness of the response, in valence and degree; and the importance of the reasons to which it is a response.

We should now reconsider the question whether unselfishness contributes to the value of motives. I shall suggest that in one sense it does, but that in a second and more important sense, it does not. Given the selfishness constraint, it is plausible that selfish motives are not *morally valuable*: they are not valuable from the moral point of view. But, having distinguished as we have between morality and reasons, there is a further question: are selfish motives *intrinsically valuable*? I suggest that they are: that a response of appropriate strength and valence to reasons involving the pleasure or pain of the agent has just the same value as being appropriately reasons-responsive as does a response of the same appropriate strength and valence to reasons involving the pleasure or pain of another being.

Suppose we have reached the best unifying account of (most of) Ross's judgments about the value of motives: that the value of motives is the product of their degree of reasons-responsiveness and of the importance of the reasons to which they respond. We should then return to the questions: Is virtue (so understood) intrinsically rather than instrumentally valuable? And is it (as Ross in various ways wants to suggest) of much greater intrinsic value than pleasure and pain?

To argue that virtue as Ross conceives it is intrinsically rather than merely instrumentally valuable, we might draw on Thomas Hurka's treatment of virtue. Hurka develops a recursive account of virtue: the idea that virtue and vice are to be understood as a matter of appropriate or inappropriate (positive or negative) attitudes to goods and evils. He argues plausibly that the value of fitting attitudes to base goods and evils is intrinsic, not merely instrumental. His case for this view is developed at length in *Virtue, Vice, and Value*;[12] summarizing in *British Ethical Theorists from Sidgwick to Ewing*, he writes:[13]

> The principles defining virtue and vice, for example that it is good to love what is good, are intuitively appealing in the abstract, as are their implications and the way the principles explain them. (BET 221)

Ross's view is in significant part a version of the recursive account. For most of the motives Ross considers fit the recursive model; and we can appeal to that model to argue that they have intrinsic value.

In one way, then, Hurka's arguments help Ross: they help the case that the value of virtue is intrinsic, not merely instrumental. But in another way they threaten Ross's view. As we saw earlier, Ross claims (in different ways in *The Right and the Good* and the *Foundations*) that virtue is the greatest good. By contrast, Hurka argues that virtue is a lesser good. As he articulates the claim,

> Far from being the greatest good, virtue is in the following sense a lesser good: the value of a virtuous attitude to a good or evil object is always less than the value, either positive or negative, of that object. (*Virtue, Vice, and Value*, 129)

The initial argument for the claim that virtue is a lesser good involves cases where we add to a situation (i) a base evil like pain, and (ii) a virtuous attitude to that base evil: hating the pain. The intuition is that doing so will always make a situation worse: the goodness of the virtuous attitude to a pain cannot compensate for the badness of the pain. This intuition is captured in a general comparative principle about the values of attitudes and their objects:

> (CP) The degree of intrinsic goodness or evil of an attitude to x is always less than the degree of goodness or evil of x. (*Virtue, Vice, and Value*, 133)

Suppose we accept (CP). Does it follow that virtue as Ross conceives it is in Hurka's sense a lesser good? Not straightforwardly. For in one crucial way Ross departs from the recursive model. What Ross regards as the most valuable motive, the desire to do one's duty, does not fit the model: for though Ross thinks the most valuable motive is the desire to do one's duty, he denies that doing one's duty is intrinsically good.

One might however try to extend Hurka's argument to show that Rossian virtue too is a lesser good. In doing so one could first endorse an anti-Rossian principle Hurka articulates; call it (AR):

> (AR) Ross holds that conscientiousness is the highest virtue, higher even than intellectualized love of the good, but I see no reason for this view. If a person acts simultaneously from a desire to do what is right and a desire to produce the most good, believing that the two coincide, his two motives seem to me of equal value. (*Virtue, Vice, and Value*, 213)

The argument would then be that, even for Ross, doing one's duty partly involves producing good. By (CP), the degree of intrinsic goodness of a desire to produce the most good is less than the degree of goodness of what produces the most good. And by (AR), the desire to do one's duty is no more valuable than the desire to produce the most good. Hence the desire to do one's duty is less valuable than the good produced in doing one's duty.

There are enough potential problems in this revised argument that I would not rely on it and confidently claim that Rossian virtue is a lesser good. But I think the argument is still important. For it helps support the weaker conclusion we came to by an independent route in sections 3 and 4: that there is no good reason to endorse Ross's radical antihedonism. Pleasure and virtue are (in the relevant rough sense, contra Ross) equally valuable.

Ross is initially inclined to put knowledge in the middle of the hierarchy—to make it a greater good than pleasure but a lesser good than virtue. Given that, as we have just argued, virtue and pleasure are roughly equally valuable, there is no remaining space or motivation for claims about the greater or lesser value of knowledge. If it is intrinsically valuable, knowledge too must be, in the same rough sense, as valuable as pleasure and virtue. I now turn to Ross's account of the value of knowledge.

5. ROSS ON THE VALUE OF KNOWLEDGE

Ross devotes considerably less attention to knowledge than he does to virtue; as he remarks (RG 145), the commensuration of different states of knowledge against each other had been much less discussed by his predecessors than had the commensuration of pleasures.

His views are framed by the distinctive form of knowledge-first epistemology he inherits from Cook Wilson and Prichard:[14]

> Knowledge . . . and right opinion . . . are not species of a single genus. Knowledge is apprehension of fact, and right opinion is not that, but is simply a state of mind in which things are believed (*not* apprehended) to be related as they are in fact related. We cannot say that knowledge and right opinion are species of a single genus (say 'cognition'), differing in degree of certainty; for knowledge alone has certainty, and opinion has merely varying degrees of approach to certainty. (RG 146)

Ross distinguishes three kinds of state with decreasing degrees of epistemic value: insight or understanding, (mere) factual knowledge, and right opinion.

> Knowledge of mere matters of fact (say of the number of stories in a building), without knowledge of their relation to

other facts, might seem to be worthless; it certainly seems to be worth much less than the knowledge of general principles, or of facts as depending on general principles—what we might call insight or understanding as opposed to mere knowledge. But on reflection it seems clear that even about matters of fact right opinion is in itself a better state of mind to be in than wrong, and knowledge than right opinion. (RG 139)

His intuitions here seem to me right.

Contemporary epistemologists have devoted much more attention than did Ross's interlocutors to questions about the value of knowledge. The problem why knowledge is more valuable than mere true belief has been labeled "the value problem."[15] The problem takes a distinctive form in the context of knowledge-first views like Ross's. For then no answer can be had by finding the extra component that turns true belief into knowledge (justification, justification plus, or whatever) and arguing that this is the source of the distinctive extra value of knowledge. But we can still ask what it is that makes a state of knowing some fact intrinsically better than a state of (mere) right opinion about that same fact.

Ross suggests two reasons. First,

Knowledge is either the direct non-inferential apprehension of fact, or the inferential apprehension of one fact as necessitated by other facts, while opinion is never either completely non-inferential or completely inferential, but is always the holding of a view which is partly grounded on apprehension of fact and partly the product of other psychical events such as wishes, hopes, fears, or the mere association of ideas. (RG 148)

This does not seem right. Ross writes as if (mere) right opinion is always the product of some intellectual vice. But surely there are many situations in which right opinion about some fact is all that is available even to those who fully exercise and only exercise epistemic virtues. Suppose, in line with the very best sports analytics, I believe that Arsenal will beat Hull tomorrow morning; and my credence is 70%. Suppose Arsenal do indeed beat Hull tomorrow. This seems a matter about which the best I can do right now is to have right opinion. And that right opinion need not reflect any intellectual deficiency.

The second reason Ross gives is

> Knowledge differs from and is superior to opinion [due to] certainty or complete absence of doubt. But we cannot say that opinion approximates in value to knowledge in proportion as it approaches to certainty. It rises in value not by being held with more conviction, but by being held with a degree of conviction which answers more closely to the degree to which the opinion is grounded on knowledge. . . . To misestimate the probability of our opinions is equally bad, whether we overestimate or underestimate it. (RG 148)

Here again the argument seems unpersuasive. At least if the point is again a matter of epistemic virtue, it seems just as virtuous to have appropriate probabilistic conviction about matters with respect to which we have limited evidence as it is to be certain of matters about which we have conclusive evidence. Right now I am thinking exactly rightly in assigning a 70% probability to Arsenal beating Hull tomorrow. I am exercising my intellectual faculties just as well here as I am in my certainty that Arsenal lost last week against Chelsea. Again, Ross's idea seems to be that what makes right opinion *in general* (as opposed to lucky or ill-grounded right opinion) less valuable than knowledge is that it involves some intellectual vice. But, as the example again illustrates and as Ross in effect admits in the passage, this need not be so.

The general problem here is that Ross's inherited epistemological view leaves no room, or anyway insufficient room, for epistemic luck. This comes out in an earlier passage. Ross remarks,

> While opinion recognized to be such is never thoroughly satisfactory to its possessor, there is another state of mind which is not knowledge—which may yet even be mistaken—yet which through lack of reflection is not distinguished from knowledge by its possessor, the state of mind which Professor Cook Wilson has called "that of being under the impression that so-and-so is the case." Such a state of mind may be as great a source of satisfaction to its possessor as knowledge, yet we should all think it to be an inferior state of mind to knowledge. (RG 139–40)

In the current context, what is striking about this passage is the assumption that such states can always be distinguished from knowledge through reflection. This idea—that if S knows P then S knows that S knows that P, or that knowledge is transparent—is specifically rejected by contemporary knowledge-first epistemologists like Williamson, and seems partly to explain Ross's problematic claims about what makes knowledge better than mere right opinion.[16]

Ross's views about what makes insight or understanding more valuable than mere knowledge seem to me considerably more plausible than his claims about what makes knowledge more valuable than mere right opinion. He says, citing Bradley,

> Knowledge of general principles is intellectually more valuable than knowledge of isolated matters of fact. . . . Our ideal in

> the pursuit of knowledge is system, and system involves the
> tracing of consequents to their ultimate grounds. (RG 147)

Thus Ross articulates (what seem to me) plausible claims about the relative value of insight or understanding, (mere) factual knowledge, and right opinion. His sketch of the reasons why insight or understanding is more valuable than (mere) factual knowledge is also promising. But he does less well in answering his version of the value question: he does not adequately explain why knowledge is more valuable than right opinion.

6. THE COMPREHENSIVENESS OF ROSS'S LIST

Turn now to the question whether Ross is right in tentatively claiming in *The Right and the Good* that his list of intrinsic goods is exhaustive. As he puts it

> I am unable to discover anything that is intrinsically good,
> which is not either one of these or a combination of two or
> more of them. (RG 140)

I shall endorse a weaker but related claim: not that Ross's list of intrinsic goods is exhaustive, but that it is the right starting place for a list of intrinsic goods, in two senses: that no good other than those Ross enumerates has a stronger claim to be on the list than they do; and that he supplies an attractive framework for assessing other candidate intrinsic goods.

Begin with the plausibility of the view that happiness, virtue, and knowledge have the strongest claim to be the basic items on the list. Here we can appeal to Sidgwick's claim, quoted above, that

> *Prima facie* the only two ends which have a strongly and widely supported claim to be regarded as rational ultimate ends are.... Happiness and Perfection. (ME 9)

If we understand perfection as having two dimensions— moral perfection and intellectual perfection—we generate just Ross's list of basic goods.

Relatedly, Ross himself gives a tentative argument for the exhaustiveness of his list of basic goods:

> This list . . . perhaps derives some support from the fact that it harmonizes with a widely accepted classification of the elements of the life of the soul. It is usual to enumerate these as cognition, feeling, and conation. Now knowledge is the ideal state of the mind . . . on the cognitive . . . side; pleasure is its ideal state on the side of feeling; and virtue is its ideal state on the side of conation; while the allocation of happiness to virtue is a good which we recognize when we reflect on the ideal relation between the conative side and the side of feeling. (RG 140)

To put this into more familiar modern terminology: the basic distinct kinds of mental states are beliefs, desires, and feelings. Given the view (that Ross shares with Sidgwick) that "Ultimate Good can only be conceived as Desirable Consciousness" (ME 398), it is very natural to begin by thinking, as Ross does in the passage above, that there is one intrinsic good for each kind of conscious state.

Independently of Ross, one could also try arguing for the basic three items on the list—pleasure, virtue, and knowledge—by appeal to Robert Nozick's experience machine thought experiment.[17] The thought experiment invites us to begin by assuming that pleasure or pain—how our life feels from the inside—is *one* of the things that matters intrinsically. And Nozick describes what is missing in a life in the experience machine in ways that might be taken to support Ross's moderate pluralism. One kind of thing that is missing in a life in the experience machine is that we don't really *do* things, and that we care that we *are* a certain way. These ideas might be taken to support the claim that virtue is intrinsically valuable.[18] Another thing missing in a life in the experience machine is contact with reality. This might be taken to support the claim that knowledge is intrinsically valuable.

Ross's view about the comprehensiveness of his list and about other candidate intrinsic goods changed significantly between *The Right and the Good* and the *Foundations*. In *The Right and the Good* he was committed, at least tentatively, to the exhaustiveness of his list of intrinsic goods and so to treating any other intrinsic goods as complex compounds of virtue, knowledge, and pleasure:

> Of the three elements virtue, knowledge, and pleasure are compounded all the complex states of mind that we think good in themselves. Aesthetic enjoyment, for example, seems to be a blend of pleasure with insight into the nature of the object that inspires it. (RG 141)

By contrast, in the *Foundations* he is prepared to treat artistic *activity* as a distinct intrinsic good:

> [Artistic creation], like knowledge, appears to be good . . . in the sense that it is an admirable activity of the human spirit; and it owes its goodness to its own intrinsic character. (F 270)

And at the start of Lecture XI he remarks that things that are good in the sense of being worthy objects of admiration are not all as such morally good:

> Excellent scientific or artistic activity is good but not morally good. (F 290)

These changes in Ross's view seem to me helpful. For the inclusion of goods of activity in the framework in the *Foundations* allows for a response to an important objection. Thomas Hurka consistently argues that achievement is an intrinsic good.[19] And he remarks of Ross (and Rashdall and Ewing),

> Rashdall, Ross, and Ewing . . . affirmed goods of feeling, cognition, and conation, with virtue the good of the latter; since they recognized just one good per faculty, that . . . left no room for achievement. (BET 210)

This passage is right about Ross's view in *The Right and the Good*. But it doesn't fit his view in the *Foundations*. As we just saw, Ross there allows for goods of activity; and he allows for multiple distinct forms of good activity (theoretical and aesthetic). So his view in the *Foundations* does leave room for a further distinct good of achievement (of which artistic creation might turn out to be one subvariety).

I suggest that the most plausible Rossian view about the range of intrinsic goods should include elements from both *The Right and the Good* and the *Foundations*. We should begin, as Ross does in *The Right and the Good* with an inventory of kinds of mental state or of mental faculties: belief, desire, and feeling. For each of these there is a single kind of intrinsic good, knowledge, virtue, and pleasure. And these are the intrinsic goods with the strongest claim to inclusion. But there are also, as he recognizes in the *Foundations*, multiple possible distinct goods of activity: these may include the good of artistic creation as well as a more generic good of achievement. And these goods of activity are not, in the way desert is, compound goods; their value is not explicable as a combination of valuable elements of pleasure, knowledge, and virtue.

7. CLASSICAL DEONTOLOGY: SKETCH OF A NORMATIVE THEORY

In the last three chapters we have gradually developed a normative theory. We began with Ross's most famous conceptual innovation: the concept of prima facie duty. We then turned to the critique of ideal utilitarianism, and highlighted the idea of special obligations as agent-relative intensifiers of reasons to produce particular goods. We finally considered Ross's moderate pluralism about the good.

The normative theory at which we have arrived—classical deontology—can be summarized in four propositions: (1) claims about prima facie duties should be reinterpreted as claims about normative reasons; (2) there is a prima facie duty to produce what is intrinsically good; (3) four things are intrinsically good: virtue, knowledge, pleasure, and the allocation of pleasure to virtue; there may also be further goods of achievement; (4) three kinds of facts recognized by Ross are agent-relative intensifiers of reasons to produce goods: facts about promises made, about past harms, and about past benefits. And one other kind of fact recognized by

Sidgwick but not Ross is also an agent-relative intensifier: the fact that a pleasure or pain will accrue to the agent.

As we have seen, Ross says his list of kinds of prima facie duty is "provisional" (RG 22) and does not claim for it "completeness or finality" (RG 20). Classical deontology's list of kinds of intrinsic goods and kinds of agent-relative intensifiers should be understood as provisional in the same way. Classical deontology is compatible with the possibility that there are further distinct kinds of intrinsic good beyond those enumerated in (3); and it is compatible with the possibility that there are further distinct kinds of facts which are agent-relative intensifiers beyond those enumerated in (4).

NOTES

1. It did, of course, as Ross himself was first to admit, develop ideas of Prichard's. But, as is characteristic in such cases, Ross developed the ideas much more fully and clearly than Prichard ever did.
2. For Moore, see *Principia Ethica*, especially chapters 3 and 6. For Rashdall see *The Theory of Good and Evil* (Oxford: Oxford University Press, 1907).
3. In giving this argument, Ross in effect denies that the intrinsic value of a world is simply the sum of the intrinsic values of its base goods. Desert for Ross is a higher-order good. He thinks it is the main genuine instance of Moore's doctrine of organic unities (RG 69–73; F 185–86). In "Rossian Totalism about Intrinsic Value," *Philosophical Studies* 173 (2016): 2069–86, Luis Oliveira argues that there is a more systematic way, inspired by Ross, to reject the assumption that the intrinsic value of a world is the sum of the intrinsic values of its base goods, and that if we systematically reject this assumption we may be able to avoid Parfit's repugnant conclusion.
4. On page 206 of *British Ethical Theorists from Sidgwick to Ewing*, Hurka denies that Ross thinks knowledge is infinitely superior

to pleasure. He writes: "[Knowledge's] value was especially emphasized by Rashdall and Ross. . . . They did not think it infinitely better than pleasure. . . . But they both thought knowledge is generally preferable to pleasure and thus the greatest non-moral good" (RG 151–52). Ross's discussion of this matter is brief and could be understood as Hurka does. But, it seems to me, the balance of the textual evidence is against Hurka's reading. On page 150 Ross initially treats the argument from the impossibility of finding a precise equivalent in terms of pleasure for some amount of virtue as applying to knowledge too. And on 151–52 he says that, though it would be paradoxical to say that the slightest possible increase in knowledge would outweigh great loss of pleasure if "knowledge [is] considered simply as a condition of intellect," it is not so given that "most (if not all) states of knowledge" are the "actualization of a virtuous desire." And he goes on to characterize his view (again, assimilating virtue and knowledge) as the view "that virtue and knowledge are much better things than pleasure" (152). Ross more straightforwardly (though tentatively) endorses the lexical priority of virtue over knowledge: "when we turn to consider the relative value of moral goodness and knowledge as ends, here again I am inclined to think that moral goodness is infinitely better than knowledge" (152).

5. There are two important recent discussions of these parts of Ross which come to conflicting conclusions—Philip Stratton-Lake's "Pleasure and Reflection in Ross's Intuitionism," in Stratton-Lake, ed., *Ethical Intuitionism: Re-evaluations* (Oxford: Oxford University Press, 2002), 113–36, and Robert Shaver's "Ross on Self and Others," *Utilitas* 26.3 (2014): 303–20. As Shaver helpfully presents him (303), Ross suggests a trilemma:

(i) Innocent pleasure is good as an end.
(ii) I have a prima facie duty to produce what is good as an end.
(iii) I have no prima facie duty to produce innocent pleasure for myself.

In *The Right and the Good* Ross denies (iii), while in the *Foundations* he denies (i). Stratton-Lake defends Ross's solution in the *Foundations*—to deny (i). Shaver argues for rejecting (ii). Shaver's argument for rejecting (ii) depends importantly on understanding "prima facie duty" as distinctively moral, and not equivalent to "normative reason." As will be clear from the above, I am much more in sympathy with Shaver's position on this issue.

6. Ross also treats disinterestedness as a distinguishing feature of the moral in his account of the development of the idea of duty (F 169–71).

7. It is also possible to think—as Moore did in *Principia*—that only the concept of intrinsic goodness is fundamental. But then (as Moore's example illustrates) the consequentialist claim has to be the whole truth, not part of the truth, about rightness.

8. For Kant see (of course) the *Grundlegung* AK 397–400 (a familiar edition is Immanuel Kant, *Grounding for the Metaphysics of Morals*, tr. James W. Ellington [Indianapolis, IN: Hackett, 1993]). Ross discusses Kant's treatment on pages 14–18 of *Kant's Ethical Theory* (Oxford: Clarendon Press, 1954) as well as in chapter 7 of *The Right and the Good* and Lecture XII of the *Foundations*.

9. For relevant parts of Butler see particularly the preface and Sermon XI in Joseph Butler, *Fifteen Sermons & Other Writings on Ethics*, ed. David McNaughton (Oxford: Oxford University Press, 2017). Ross's admiration for Butler is evidenced, inter alia, by the long quotation on pages 78–79 of the *Foundations*.

10. "Finally, we must compare the desire to do one's duty, both in its particularized and in its generalized form, with all the other motives I have named. It seems to me clear that in either form it ranks above all other motives" (F 303).

11. Bernard Williams, "Persons, Character and Morality," in *Moral Luck* (Cambridge: Cambridge University Press, 1981), 18.

12. Thomas Hurka, *Virtue, Vice, and Value* (Oxford: Oxford University Press, 2001). Page references will be placed in the text.

13. I will refer to *British Ethical Theorists* as "BET"; page references will be placed in the text.

14. For Cook Wilson, see John Cook Wilson, *Statement and Inference*, 2 vols. (Oxford: Clarendon Press, 1926). For

Prichard see H. A. Prichard, *Knowledge and Perception* (Oxford: Clarendon Press, 1950) and *Moral Writings*.

15. For a survey, see Duncan Pritchard, "Recent Work on Epistemic Value," *American Philosophical Quarterly* 44.2 (2007): 85–110. Pritchard distinguishes the primary value problem—the problem why knowledge is more valuable than mere true belief—from the secondary value problem—the problem why knowledge is more valuable than any proper subset of its parts.

16. For Williamson's own view, see Timothy Williamson, *Knowledge and Its Limits* (Oxford: Oxford University Press, 2000). For his take on Prichard, see in particular the following passage from page 23: "H.A. Prichard, who also took knowing to be a mental state, held that one is always in a position to know whether one knows or merely believes. . . . Few now would claim such powers of discrimination."

17. Robert Nozick, *Anarchy, State, and Utopia* (New York: Basic Books, 1974), 42–45.

18. It might be objected that virtue as Ross understands it can be instantiated in an experience machine. For Rossian virtue, as we saw in section 4, is simply a matter of the objects of our desires. And individuals in experience machines do, or anyway can, have genuine desires.

    On this matter, what Nozick himself says is "A second reason for not plugging in is that we want to *be* a certain way, to be a certain sort of person. Someone floating in a tank is an indeterminate blob. There is no answer to the question of what a person is like who has long been in the tank. Is he courageous, kind, intelligent, witty, loving? It's not merely that it's difficult to tell: there's no way he is. Plugging into the machine is a kind of suicide" (43).

    While Nozick does not in this passage conceive of what someone is like solely as a matter of the objects of his or her desires, the passage does suggest that Nozick thinks that there is no truth about the kind of desires a person long in the machine has. If so, Nozick would reject the claim that Rossian virtue can be instantiated in an experience machine.

19. In both *Virtue, Vice, and Value* and *British Ethical Theorists*. For a full treatment of the value of achievement, see Gwen Bradford, *Achievement* (Oxford: Oxford University Press, 2015).

5

THE METAETHICAL

AND EPISTEMOLOGICAL

FRAMEWORK

IN *THE RIGHT AND THE Good* and the *Foundations*, Ross develops and relies on an explicit metaethical and epistemological framework in arguing for his key normative conclusions. My topic in this final chapter is that metaethical and epistemological framework.

It is widely recognized that Ross's most important innovation in normative theory is the introduction of the concept of prima facie duty, whose character we discussed in chapter 2. I shall argue that the most important distinctive features of Ross's metaethics also involve this concept. Specifically, what is novel in his nonnaturalist metaethical framework is the emphasis on the distinction between essence theories and grounds theories. And his most distinctive claim in moral epistemology is a claim about the epistemic status of principles of prima facie duty or grounds claims.

I will largely defend this metaethical framework and Ross's presentation of the case for nonnaturalism. I will argue that the systematic deployment of the distinction between essence theories and grounds theories is illuminating, and in particular a significant advance on the metaethical framework employed by Moore in *Principia*. I will claim that Ross does well in offering appropriately nuanced arguments for nonnaturalism. I will claim that he does well too in recognizing and taking on two new alternative positions in metaethics: the early noncognitivism advocated by Ayer and Carnap;[1] and error theory, which, at the time he wrote the *Foundations*, had no unequivocal advocates. Insofar as there are problems in Ross's metaethics, these problems involve grounds theories: Ross fails to notice the best strategy of argument for monistic grounds theories, and assimilates the strategy of argument against grounds theories too closely to the strategy of argument against essence theories.

I will argue that Ross's moral epistemology is more problematic. That moral epistemology has two particularly notable features. The first is a commitment to a distinctive form of knowledge-first epistemology inherited from Cook Wilson and Prichard.[2] The second is a striking epistemic asymmetry claim, framed in terms of this distinctive epistemology: the claim that judgments of prima facie duty are objects of knowledge while judgments of duty proper are objects of mere opinion. A question about the distinctive epistemology is whether it leads to dogmatism. I will argue that in Prichard's case it does: Prichard is strikingly and wrongly more dogmatic than Sidgwick. It is unclear how far Prichard here influenced Ross. But I will argue that, in any event, the epistemic asymmetry claim is problematic: when we reflect on our grounds convictions or convictions as to principles of prima facie duty, we cannot plausibly maintain that they always meet Prichard's and Ross's standards for knowledge; and nor can we maintain that our degree of warrant in holding these convictions is always greater than our degree of warrant in holding other sorts of convictions that generate judgments of duty proper, most importantly convictions as to the relative weight of different prima facie duties.

1. ESSENCE THEORIES AND GROUNDS THEORIES

The most important distinctive feature of Ross's metaethics is the systematic deployment of the distinction between essence theories and grounds theories. He introduces the distinction by reflection on the example of hedonism and the question whether it is a naturalistic or a nonnaturalistic theory:

> At first sight Hedonism . . . would seem to belong to the class of naturalistic theories about rightness, and it is often so described—described as "reducing" rightness to the tendency to produce pleasure. But we must be careful to distinguish two possibilities. A hedonist may take the view that this is what rightness *is*, that this is its correct definition; and then he is offering a naturalistic theory. But he may be holding something quite different. He may be holding that rightness is something indefinable, and merely claiming that that which *makes* acts right is their tendency to promote pleasure. Then he is holding that a non-ethical characteristic, a psychological characteristic, is the ground of rightness but not its essence. And if so the theory . . . is not a naturalistic theory. (F 8–9)

This distinction is required once you introduce, as of course Ross does in *The Right and the Good*, the concept of prima facie duty. For you then have to distinguish, as the

titles of the first two chapters of *The Right and the Good*
make clear, between questions as to "the meaning of 'right'"
and questions as to "what makes right acts right." But it is
in the *Foundations* that Ross deploys the distinction more
systematically. Principles of prima facie duty may be alternately labeled "grounds principles." They are principles as to
what properties ground rightness or make acts right. It is also
natural to make the same distinction with respect to goodness: the distinction between questions as to the meaning
or essence of goodness and questions as to what properties
ground goodness or make things good. Grounds theories
(with respect either to rightness or to goodness) can then be
either monistic or pluralistic: they can say that there is a single
ground of rightness or goodness, or multiple grounds. And
once the distinction is made it is also natural to ask about the
character of the arguments for grounds principles, and about
the epistemic status of our convictions as to grounds principles: How can we argue for or against grounds principles or
grounds theories, and how far should these arguments resemble arguments for or against essence theories? And what
degree of certainty or credence can we properly hope to ob-
tain in our convictions as to grounds principles and grounds
theories?

The utility of the distinction between essence theories
and grounds theories can be illustrated historically. It allows
us to frame two problematic and controversial features of
the metaethics of Moore's *Principia* much more satisfactorily
than Moore is himself there able to do. Readers of the first
chapter of *Principia*, especially those influenced by contemporary metaethics to expect to find in it "the open question
argument," will be surprised that the term "open question" occurs only once in the chapter.[3] The concept Moore

emphasizes instead is "the naturalistic fallacy." As has been generally accepted at least since Frankena's famous article[4] (and was probably accepted earlier than that by Moore himself),[5] the naturalistic fallacy is not a fallacy. But there is still the question just what kind of mistake Moore, in talking about the naturalistic fallacy, supposes the naturalist to make. There are some quite implausible suggestions in *Principia*, most implausibly the suggestion in section 12 of the first chapter that naturalists confuse the 'is' of identity with the 'is' of predication. The distinction between essence claims and grounds claims allows for a much more plausible account of the mistake naturalists are allegedly making (though it is still of course not a fallacy): their mistake is to confuse grounds claims with essence claims.

And, indeed, in discussing the evolutionary or sociological school, Ross provides an example of thinkers committing the naturalistic fallacy in this sense; an example arguably more persuasive than Moore's own diagnoses of Bentham and Mill (*Principia*, 17–19 and 64–74):

> The evolutionary and sociological school of thought has on the whole shown little if any awareness of the distinction between two questions which are logically entirely different [the question as to the essence of rightness and the question as to the ground of rightness]. . . . The method usually followed by this school is to pass under review a variety of types of act that are commonly called right; to find, or argue, that they have some characteristic in common, e.g., that of being comparatively highly evolved; and then to assume that that is what 'right' or 'obligatory' means. But it is clear that, assuming the review of instances to be adequate . . . two possibilities remain. The common characteristic thus discovered may be what we mean by 'right'; or it may be a characteristic on which rightness is

consequent but which is itself different from rightness; not the essence of rightness, but its ground. (F 12)

Relatedly, we can deploy the distinction between essence theories and grounds theories to make sense of Moore's confusing claim that while goodness cannot be defined, "the good" can:

> But I am afraid that I have still not removed the chief difficulty which may prevent acceptance of the proposition that good is indefinable. I do not mean to say that *the* good, that which is good, is thus indefinable; if I did think so, I should not be writing on Ethics, for my main object is to help towards discovering that definition. (*Principia*, 8–9)

We can understand this confusing contrast between defining *good* and defining *the good* once we see that what Moore really means is to distinguish theories as to the essence of goodness (which he thinks cannot be given) from theories as to the grounds of goodness (which he thinks can).

And the importance of the distinction between essence theories and grounds theories is not merely historical. It plays a prominent role in the metaethics of Parfit's *On What Matters*. And it does so in a way that shows that it is not just hedonism that can be understood either as an essence theory or as a grounds theory. Parfit distinguishes two very different kinds of subjectivism about reasons. In the first five chapters of part 1, he considers and argues against subjectivism as a grounds theory: the idea, roughly, that we have reason to do whatever would best fulfill our desires. By contrast, in part 6, he argues against subjectivism as an essence theory: the view, roughly, that "reason" is *definable* in terms of desire. Parfit's treatment also shows that just as there are cases, like that of Bentham, where it is unclear whether utilitarianism is being advanced as an essence theory or a grounds theory, so there are cases, like that of Bernard Williams,[6] where it is unclear whether a desire-satisfaction theory is being advanced as an essence theory or a grounds theory.

2. ROSS'S CASE AGAINST NATURALISTIC ESSENCE THEORIES

In the introductory lecture in the *Foundations* Ross first distinguishes the right from the good:

> In the complex fabric of common opinions about moral questions two main strands may be discovered. On the one hand there is a group of opinions involving the closely connected ideas of duty, of right and wrong, of moral laws and imperatives. On the other, there are opinions involving the idea of human goods to be aimed at. (F 3)

Ross remarks that no ethical system has succeeded in eliminating either strand of thinking, and, as we have seen, it is characteristic of his own normative theorizing to give a prominent and independent place to both strands.

He turns next to the question of the definability of the key concepts, the question whether "'good' or 'right' can be elucidated without remainder in terms other than itself" (F 5). He notices two different distinctions that might be used in classifying attempts at such definitions. The first, less satisfactory distinction is between attitude and consequence theories. Attitude theories define ethical terms by reference to the attitude of some being or other; consequence theories define them by reference to total consequences. The distinction is unsatisfactory in that it "is not a logically perfect classification of the attempts to define ethical terms; for it is not based on an a priori disjunction" (F 6). The more satisfactory distinction, introduced with reference to Moore, is between naturalistic and nonnaturalistic definitions. Naturalistic definitions

> are definitions which claim to define an ethical term without using any other ethical term; [nonnaturalistic definitions] . . . are attempts to define one ethical term by the aid of another. (F 6)

The two kinds of definitions cut across one another. Thus, to take one important instance, consequence theories may be either naturalistic or nonnaturalistic. The definition of "right" as "productive of the greatest amount of pleasure" is naturalistic; the definition of "right" as "productive of the greatest amount of good" is nonnaturalistic.

Ross's treatment of naturalistic essence theories draws substantially on Moore's later writings;[7] and his treatment is in three important respects superior to Moore's famous earlier treatment in *Principia*. First, Ross does not suppose he has a single all-purpose argument against all naturalistic proposals; he thinks specific proposed analyses need to be considered individually. By contrast Moore is often read as taking himself in *Principia* to have a single all-purpose argument, involving (as we have seen) the charge that his opponents commit "the naturalistic fallacy," perhaps together with the claim that their naturalistic definitions can be shown to be mistaken by appeal to "the open question argument."[8] Second, Ross is sensitive to the possibility that we cannot in advance tell whether a concept is simple or complex, and thus that an initially surprising definition might turn out to be correct. Third, he does not claim to have established nonnaturalism definitively; he claims only to have offered a defeasible argument in its favor. All three points come out in a nice passage in the discussion of definitions of good in *The Right and the Good*:

> There seem to be cases in which we seek for the definition of a term and finally accept one as correct. The fact that we accept some definition as correct shows that the term did somehow stand for a complex of elements; yet the fact that we are for some time in doubt whether the term is analyzable, and if so, what the correct analysis is, shows that this complex of elements was not distinctly present to our mind before, or during, the search for a definition. It appears as if we cannot avoid recognizing that there is such a thing as using a term which implicitly refers to a certain complex, while yet the complex is not explicitly present to our minds. And in principle this might, it seems, be true of 'good'. The absence of an explicit reference to a complex in our ordinary use of the term should therefore not be taken as necessarily implying that the term is indefinable, nor, in particular, as excluding the possibility of its standing for a relation. The method should, I think, rather be that of attending to any proposed definition that seems at all plausible. If it is the correct definition, what should happen is that after a certain amount of attention to it we should be able to say, "yes, that is what I meant by 'good' all along, though I was not clearly conscious till now that that was what I meant." If on the other hand the result is that we feel clear that "that was not what

I meant by good," the proposed definition must be rejected.
If, after we have examined all the definitions that possess any
initial plausibility, we have found this negative result in every
case, we may feel fairly confident that 'good' is indefinable.
(92–93)

Ross devotes most attention to three kinds of naturalistic
definitions of rightness: evolutionary, attitudinal, and utilitarian. And he makes, it seems to me, three distinguishable
kinds of objection to these candidate definitions: (1) that the
definiens is not coextensive with 'right'; (2) that it is clear just
by reflection on the proposed definition that the definiens is
not what we mean by 'right'; and (3) that, though (unlike in
(2)) the definition cannot be immediately rejected, it has specific problematic consequences.

In rejecting the evolutionary definition Ross presses the
second kind of objection:

> It is surely clear that neither temporal posteriority nor com-
> plexity, nor any union of the two, is that which we mean to
> refer to when we use the term 'right' or 'obligatory'. (F 13)

In rejecting the various attitudinal definitions, by contrast,
he largely presses various objections of the third sort. Thus,
for instance, one (independently famous and not original)
ground on which he rejects the "private reaction view" on
which "X is right" means "X awakes in me the emotion of
approval" is that this view gets it wrong about when people
disagree:

> If all I mean when I say "action A is right" is "I have a feeling
> of approval towards it," and all you mean when you say "it is

wrong" is that you have a feeling of disapproval towards it,
then we are not disagreeing. (F 24)

In summarily rejecting egoistic hedonism Ross relies largely
on the first kind of objection:

> No one will have the slightest difficulty in remembering
> instances in which he has thought of some act as his duty,
> without in the least thinking of it as likely to bring him more
> pleasure than any other would. And if the two thoughts are not
> even necessarily found together, still less can it be pretended
> that they are but one thought. (F 26)

I think that on the whole Ross does a good job in
treating of naturalistic essence-theories. He allows rightly
for nonobvious definitions, he does not claim in theory to
have nor behave in practice as if he has a single master argument against all candidate definitions, and the arguments
he makes against specific naturalistic proposals, often not
arguments original with him, seem to me on the whole
persuasive. Of course, Ross could not have been expected
to anticipate, and did not anticipate, important later
developments in naturalistic metaethics. He was not in a
position to consider nonreductive naturalism of the Cornell
realist variety or the kind of reductive naturalism recently
defended by Mark Schroeder.[9] Unlike Moore and Broad,
Ross was a consistent and committed nonnaturalist: he
didn't waver between nonnaturalism and noncognitivism
when the latter came into fashion in the 1930s. The contemporary metaethicists with whom he has most in common
are thus nonnaturalists like Nagel, Parfit, and Scanlon.[10] But
it would be anachronistic to expect Ross himself directly to

supply arguments against more contemporary versions of naturalism.

3. ROSS ON NONCOGNITIVISM AND ERROR THEORY

In arguing against the naturalistic essence theories just considered Ross was (nicely, I just suggested) making a case made earlier by Moore and others. But Ross also argued strikingly against two other metaethical views which were unfamiliar when Moore wrote *Principia* but have been increasingly influential since: noncognitivism and error theory.

In the *Foundations* Ross discussed two variants of then-novel and increasingly influential noncognitivism: Ayer's and Carnap's. He suggested plausibly (F 35) that early noncognitivists were driven to their position by a need to accommodate ethical judgments within their general philosophical framework rather than by "disinterested reflection" on ethical judgments; he gave reasons to reject that general philosophical framework (35–38); and, most strikingly, he articulated a version of the "Frege-Geach" objection long before Geach:[11]

> The theory that all judgements with the predicate 'right' or 'good' are commands has evidently very little plausibility. . . . If we are to do justice to the meaning of 'right' or 'ought', we must take account also of such modes of speech as "he ought to do so-and-so," "you ought to have done so-and-so," "if this and that had been the case, you ought to have done so-and-so," "if this and that were the case, you ought to do so-and-so," "I ought to do so-and-so." Where the judgment of obligation has

> reference either to a third person, not the person addressed, or
> to the past, or to an unfulfilled past condition, or to a future
> treated as merely possible, or to the speaker himself, there is
> no plausibility in describing the judgement as a command. But
> it is easy to see that 'ought' means the same in all these cases,
> and that if in some of them it does not express a command, it
> does not do so in any. (F 33–34)

This might not be exactly be the Frege-Geach problem as
contemporary philosophers understand it. Ross targets
the objection only at Carnap's view that moral claims are
commands, not at Ayer's view that they are expressions of
attitudes; and he does not directly raise the issue of the apparent validity of arguments in which moral claims occur
in conditionals and other complex sentences. But he is
clearly enough in the same ballpark—referring explicitly to
the problem of "modes of speech" including conditionals—
that there is a historical case for relabeling the problem the
"Frege-*Ross*-Geach" problem.

Equally strikingly, Ross articulated and argued against
error theories which at that time had no explicit advocates (if
we take Mackie's 1946 article to be the earliest explicit advo-
cacy of an error theory):[12]

> So far I have been dealing with one of two alternatives, that the
> evolutionary account recognizes the existence of the attribute
> of rightness and is looking for its ground. But another alter-
> native remains. May the upshot of the evolutionary account
> be, not that obligatoriness just means evolvedness, nor that
> evolvedness is the ground of obligatoriness, but that there is
> no such thing as obligatoriness; that there is *nothing* in reality
> answering to the meaning we have in mind when we use the
> word obligatory, the only distinction that remains being that
> between less and more evolved acts? (F 15)

Moreover, Ross considered and responded to a kind of evolutionary debunking argument for error theory. He allowed for the possibility that an inquiry into the origin of a judgment might undermine its validity by showing that those who believe it have no sufficient reason for their belief (though of course the belief *might* turn out to be true). As Ross pictures it, the key idea in the evolutionary debunking argument is that distinctively moral concepts are not possessed by the lower animals from whom we evolved. The debunkers conclude that moral concepts are therefore "mere plays of fancy."

To this argument, Ross responds that the difference between human and animal thinking does not show that moral concepts are empty, any more than a similar argument shows that distinctively human mathematical concepts are empty:

Whichever account is given, we are crediting the human mind with having made at some time a new departure—either the fanciful invention of a new idea, the idea of rightness, of the detection of a hitherto undetected characteristic of actions. In either case a breach of continuity is involved, and that involved in the former case is certainly no more easy to understand than that involved in the latter. We are perfectly familiar with the fact that within the limits of a single life a mind may pass from a state in which it is quite incapable of forming certain ideas or of making certain judgements, to one in which it is capable of doing this, and we do not doubt the truth of our mature judgements because we were earlier incapable of making them; we do not for that reasons treat them as mere plays of fancy. We recognize that the truths in question—say, mathematical truths—were there all the time to be apprehended, but that a certain degree of mental maturity was necessary for their apprehension. (F 17)

And, Ross argues, we should think just the same about the mental maturation of a species over the course of evolutionary development as we do of a single individual's mental maturation over a lifetime.

It is natural to ask how much the evolutionary debunking argument Ross here considers resembles the evolutionary debunking arguments that have been much discussed in contemporary metaethics. The answer, I think, is that there is a crucial difference. In Sharon Street's influential presentation, the key premise of contemporary evolutionary debunking arguments is that evolution explains the *content* of our moral judgments: why we make the specific moral judgments we do.[13] By contrast, the key premise of the evolutionary debunking argument Ross envisages is simply that we have come (newly, at some late stage in evolutionary history) to *possess* moral concepts. So, while it is striking that Ross envisages both an error theory and an evolutionary debunking argument for it, the argument he considers is not the same as the most important arguments of its form discussed in contemporary metaethics.

4. ROSS ON ARGUMENTS FOR AND AGAINST GROUNDS THEORIES

I have argued so far that the emphasis on the distinction between essence theories and grounds theories is a distinctive positive feature of Ross's metaethics. But, I shall argue in this section, in two ways Ross doesn't take full advantage of the distinction.

The first of these we had occasion to consider in chapter 3: that Ross misses the best strategy of argument for utilitarianism, and more broadly for other monistic grounds theories. As we saw, the problem here is partly Moore's fault, and emerges in Ross's treatment of Moore. As Ross sees it, Moore's view is that what produces the maximum good is right. Initially, in *Principia*, Moore held that this consequentialist claim is true by definition. But then he (rightly) came to see that the definitional claim is false: "right" does not mean "maximally productive of good." So Moore retreats, in *Ethics*, to the corresponding grounds theory: though "right" does not *mean* "maximally productive of good," it is self-evident that "right" and "optimific" are coextensive; being optimific is the only ground of rightness.

Ross then argues against this claim. He argues first that it is not self-evident that the right coincides with the optimific. As he summarizes,

> It seems, on reflection, self-evident that a promise, simply as such, is something that *prima facie* ought to be kept, and it does *not*, on reflection, seem self-evident that production of maximum good is the only thing that makes an act obligatory. (RG 40)

The only other possibility he conceives of is that the coincidence between the right and the optimific might be established by enumerative induction, a possibility about which Ross is (rightly, it seems to me) also skeptical.

Ross here misses an alternative and better strategy of argument for ideal utilitarianism. The alternative strategy is more indirect, and ironically relies initially on a point that is central to Ross's own normative view. The point is that grounds theories need not be monistic. Characteristic grounds claims can be understood—to employ Ross's most famous concept—as claims about prima facie duty: they can be of the form: such-and-such is *a* ground of rightness, not: such-and-such is *the* ground of rightness.

The better strategy of argument for ideal utilitarianism is then two-stage and indirect. The first stage is to argue that productivity of goodness is *a* ground of rightness (a claim with which, as I have emphasized, Ross agrees). The second stage is to argue that there are no other genuine independent grounds of rightness: that all the other candidates to be independent grounds of rightness can be shown not to be. This strategy of argument does not involve establishing the truth of the claim that the right and the optimific necessarily coincide in either of the two possible ways Ross envisages (either by seeing that it is self-evident that they coincide, or that the coincidence can be established by enumerative induction). And it is, as we saw in chapter 3, surely a better account of the consequentialist strategy.

There is a second, more general issue. Ross typically moves, and moves in various particular discussions, from essence theories to grounds theories. His remarks at various points convey the impression that essence theories and grounds theories are structurally similar alternatives:

> To each of the theories I have discussed there corresponds a pair of views, each of which is more plausible than the views I have considered. Take any of the characteristics that have been put forward as giving the essence of rightness. It would be more plausible to say . . . this is the characteristic that *makes* acts right. (F 28)

Here and elsewhere, I think Ross assimilates essence theories too closely to grounds theories. It is not that he never notices important differences. As he says on pages 57–58,

I remarked before that the theories which specify this or that as the ground of rightness are in general more plausible than those which specify this or that as the essence of rightness. And in one respect this is so. For when such a characteristic as 'conducing to life' . . . is put forward as to the essence of rightness, we have only to examine what is in our mind when we say that such and such an act is right, to see that, however closely the characteristic in question may be connected with rightness, it is not the very meaning we have in mind when we assert the rightness of an act. From another point of view, some at least of the ground-theories are *less* plausible than the essence-theories. For, while, until we begin to reflect carefully on our meaning when we predicate rightness, it may seem plausible to say that rightness is just the being generally approved, for instance, it is very unplausible to say that being approved is the ground of an action's having a quite different characteristic, a characteristic of its own, that of being right.

Still, though, I will suggest, he tends to assimilate arguments against monistic grounds theories too closely to arguments against the parallel essence theories.

A general reason for caution here emerges when we reflect on Parfit's treatment of subjectivist theories. Parfit is extremely careful to distinguish the kinds of argument he offers against subjectivist grounds theories from the kind of arguments he offers against subjectivist essence theories. In particular, in arguing against subjectivism as a grounds theory, especially on pages 73–82 of volume 1 of *On What Matters*, he claims that subjectivism as a grounds theory has implausible implications. By contrast, in arguing in part 6 against subjectivism as an essence theory, he explicitly disavows any such appeal to implausible normative implications, remarking,

> It may seem that, in appealing to these imagined cases, I am trying to show that Analytical Internalism has implausible implications. But that is not my aim. (OWM 2, 281–82)

The general point here is that the kinds of argument relevant to rejecting possible grounds theories are substantially different from the kinds of argument relevant to dismissing possible essence theories. And the point clearly applies with respect to the objections Ross himself lodges against various essence theories. Of the three kinds of objections we saw Ross using against essence theories in section 2, two are clearly not directly relevant to monistic grounds theories at all. If we are considering a grounds theory, it clearly is no objection to the grounds theory that the feature presented as the ground is intuitively not what we mean by 'right'; nor does it obviously matter that features presented as grounds of rightness behave in ways that rightness itself doesn't, so much of what would fall under my category (3), that the definition has specific problematic consequences, is not relevant either.

These general problems are particularly evident in Ross's discussion of attitudinal grounds theories. Consider the argument Ross explicitly presents as an analogue of the disagreement objection which he offered against attitudinal essence theories:

> If an act is right because it is approved by A and wrong because it is disapproved by B, the same act will be in fact right and wrong. But while we might agree that the same act may be in some respects right and in others wrong, we do not suppose that the same fact can be in fact right on the whole and wrong on the whole. To think this would be to put an end to all ethical judgement. The corresponding essence-theory of rightness put an end to ethical discussion because it implied that

two men who respectively call an act right and wrong are not contradicting one another. The ground-theory puts an end to discussion because it implies that the two men are contradicting one another but nevertheless are both right. (F 60)

The first problem here is with the theory Ross is imagining. As he concedes in the passage cited, attitude theories are not particularly plausible as grounds theories in the first place; but even given that general problem, the grounds theory he is here considering is a nonstarter. Being approved by one person cannot be the sufficient ground for being right, on pain, as Ross here points out, of immediate contradiction. The grounds theory that avoids this problem will need either to relativize rightness as well as its grounds, or (more plausibly) to treat A's approval as *a* ground, not *the* ground of rightness. But that (somewhat) more plausible view is not subject to any analogue of the disagreement objection. The problem with it is not that it gets it wrong about when people disagree—for, after all, being a grounds theory, it allows for all the same disagreements as any other view that treats "right" as unanalyzable. It is rather that it is very intuitively implausible that being approved or disapproved is a feature that makes actions right or wrong.

In general, then, Ross's treatment of grounds theories is sometimes forced or unconvincing, in a way that is a product of assimilating arguments for and against grounds theories too closely to arguments for and against essence theories. Ross doesn't do enough to address the general question how we should argue for and against grounds theories, and how far those arguments ought to resemble arguments for or against parallel essence theories. Reflecting on this issue raises the question of the epistemic status of our convictions as to grounds principles, an issue central to Ross's moral epistemology.

5. ROSS'S MORAL EPISTEMOLOGY: THE CENTRAL CLAIMS

Ross's moral epistemology has two key features. First, he is committed to a distinctive kind of knowledge-first view inherited from Cook Wilson and Prichard:

> Knowledge . . . and right opinion . . . are not species of a single genus. Knowledge is apprehension of fact, and right opinion is not that, but is simply a state of mind in which things are believed (*not* apprehended) to be related as they are in fact related. We cannot say that knowledge and right opinion are species of a single genus (say 'cognition'), differing in degree of certainty; for knowledge alone has certainty, and opinion has merely varying degrees of approach to certainty. (RG 146)

Second, in *The Right and the Good* he draws a sharp distinction between the epistemic status of judgments of prima facie duty and the epistemic status of judgments of duty proper:

> Our judgments about our actual duty in concrete situations have none of the certainty that attaches to our recognition of the general principles of duty. (30)

This claim is fleshed out in striking passages on pages 28–34 of *The Right and the Good*. Two passages in particular stand out:

> Something should be said of the relation between our apprehension of the *prima facie* rightness of certain types of act and our mental attitude towards particular acts. It is proper to use

the word 'apprehension' in the former case and not in the latter. That an act, *qua* fulfilling a promise, or *qua* effecting a just distribution of good, or *qua* returning services rendered, or *qua* promoting the good of others, or *qua* promoting the virtue or insight of the agent, is *prima facie* right is self-evident; not in the sense that it is evident from the beginning of our lives, or as soon as we attend to the proposition for the first time, but in the sense that when we have reached sufficient mental maturity and have given sufficient attention to the proposition it is evident without any need of proof, or of evidence beyond itself. It is self-evident just as a mathematical axiom, or the validity of a form of inference, is evident. The moral order expressed in these propositions is just as much part of the fundamental nature of the universe (and, we may add, of any possible universe in which there were moral agents at all) as is the spatial or numerical structure expressed in the axioms of geometry or arithmetic. (29–30)

Shortly afterward he explicitly contrasts the self-evidence of judgments of prima facie duty with the lesser epistemic status of judgments of duty proper:

Our judgments about our actual duty in concrete situations have none of the certainty that attaches to our recognition of the general principles of duty. A statement is certain, i.e. is an expression of knowledge, only in one or other of two cases: when it is either self-evident, or a valid conclusion from self-evident premises. And our judgements about our particular duties have neither of these characters. (1) They are not self-evident. Where a possible act is seen to have two characteristics, in virtue of one of which it is *prima facie* right, and in virtue of the other *prima facie* wrong, we are (I think) well aware that we are not certain whether we ought or ought not to do it; that whether we do it or not, we are taking a moral risk. We come in the long run, after consideration, to think one duty more pressing than the other, but we do not feel certain that it is so. (2) Again, our judgements about our particular duties are not logical conclusions from self-evident premises. (RG 30–31)

I will begin with the first distinctive feature: with the question whether Ross's commitment to the general epistemological position inherited from Cook-Wilson and Prichard makes him objectionably dogmatic. I will then ask whether, whatever its source, the epistemic asymmetry claim is defensible. In doing so I will be, in key part, asking a question that arises naturally once one distinguishes essence claims and theories from grounds claims and theories by introducing the concept of prima facie duty: what is the epistemic status of grounds principles (which are or which include principles of prima facie duty)?

6. FALLIBILISM AND DOGMATISM: PRICHARD, SIDGWICK, AND ROSS

As I argued above, Ross's nonnaturalist metaethics is a sophisticated version of views developed earlier by Moore; and (as is widely recognized, though I did not have space to argue for it) Moore's views derive from and importantly resemble Sidgwick's. But it is not so clear that Ross's views in moral epistemology are the same as Sidgwick's. As Hurka writes,

> Some commentators have contrasted Sidgwick's fallibilism with the allegedly more dogmatic views of later writers such as . . . Prichard . . . and Ross; this is meant to be another

case where insights of Sidgwick were lost. But the contrast is . . . overdrawn, since many of those later writers likewise insisted that intuition is fallible. (BET 115)

I shall first argue here, contra Hurka, that the commentators he mentions are in one important way right. There is a real contrast between Prichard and Sidgwick: Prichard is strikingly more dogmatic than Sidgwick.[14] I will then ask whether the same is true of Ross.

Start with a sketch of Sidgwick's fallibilist position in the *Methods*. It is crucial to the project of the methods to apply to putatively self-evident moral axioms

Four conditions, the complete fulfilment of which would establish a significant proposition, apparently self-evident, in the highest degree of certainty attainable: and which must be approximately realised by the premises of our reasoning in any inquiry if that reasoning is to lead us cogently to trustworthy conclusions. (ME 338)

The four conditions are

1. The terms of the proposition must be clear and precise.
2. The self-evidence of the proposition must be ascertained by careful reflection.
3. The propositions accepted as self-evident must be mutually consistent.
4. No epistemic peer must disagree that the proposition is self-evident.

Sidgwick appeals to these conditions in arguing against dogmatic intuitionism and in favor of utilitarianism. Whether he manages to do so in a way that is fair and convincing is a further question (to which I think the answer is no).[15] But, either way, the conditions are crucial to the argument of the *Methods*.

The conditions are presented somewhat abruptly in the *Methods*. But Sidgwick discusses and applies what seem to be the same conditions more fully in his articles in general and moral epistemology. He characteristically begins the articles in general epistemology with the problem of error:

> Ordinary thinking . . . affirms propositions, both general and individual, in great number and of various kinds. But in the progress of thought some of these are recognized as erroneous. . . . To the reflective or philosophic mind the ascertained erroneousness of some beliefs suggests the possible erroneousness of all. . . . The radical, general, justification of . . . natural skepticism is the admitted fact of error. A belief which I held certainly true, I now find doubtful or even false; what then guarantees me against a similar discovery as to all the other beliefs which I am now holding true?[16]

Sidgwick's response to the challenge is to consider criteria of truth and error. As he characterizes the strategy:

> The mode in which dogmatists have tried to supply such a guarantee is by the establishment of a criterion or criteria of truth; by pointing out certain characteristics of true beliefs, which, it is asserted, have never been possessed by beliefs that have been found false.[17]

Sidgwick argues that there is no infallible criterion:

> On the whole, then, I have to reject the claims of Empiricism no less than of Rationalism to put forward a simple infallible

criterion of the kind of knowledge which is to be taken as the ultimately valid basis of all else that is commonly taken for knowledge. I regard both criteria as *useful*, as a means of guarding against error, but neither as infallible. I propose, then, to turn from infallible criteria to what I call methods of verification: from the search after an absolute test of truth to the humbler task of excluding error.[18]

On Sidgwick's view certainty comes in degrees, and we can never rule out the possibility of error even in propositions that seem to us self-evident. All we can do is to employ the criteria to raise the level of certainty:

> A proposition which presents itself to my mind as self-evident, and is in harmony with all the rest of my intuitions relating to the same subject, and is also ascertained to be accepted by all other minds that have been led to contemplate it, may after all turn out to be false: but it seems to have as high a degree of certainty as I can hope to obtain under the existing conditions of human thought.[19]

Sidgwick's fallibilism in moral philosophy is thus a product of a more general fallibilism. Sidgwick thinks that apparently intuitive propositions can turn out to be false; and that the best way to guard against the danger of falsity is to employ criteria of truth and error.

Prichard's treatment of the same issues could hardly present a starker contrast. Like Sidgwick, Prichard begins with the problem of error; and, like Sidgwick in his articles in general epistemology, in *Knowledge and Perception* Prichard raises the problem while discussing Descartes.

> Descartes says to himself: I have spent much of my life in the endeavor to gain knowledge in various directions. . . . As the

result I have acquired a number of convictions on matters of all kinds. But two reflections suggest that possibly *all* my existing convictions may be false. The first is that I have frequently turned out to be mistaken even on matters that seemed to me certain. (*Knowledge and Perception*, 74)

Like Sidgwick, Prichard considers the possibility of appealing to a criterion or criteria of truth. But while Sidgwick embraces (a nuanced version of) this possibility, Prichard rejects any appeal to it as "fallacious":

[Descartes's fallacious] idea is that by analyzing the process by which he has become certain of his own existence, he can discover the general nature of the process of becoming certain of something, and that once we know its general nature, we can use this knowledge to attain other certainties. (*Knowledge and Perception*, 80)

Prichard's own solution is quite different. He thinks that the proper approach to the argument from error is to treat the initial doubt that drives it as misconceived. We cannot properly doubt anything we know. If we know, we do or can know that we know. We can only begin to doubt by exiting this state of knowledge; and at that point the doubt cannot be allayed. The only remedy is to get back into the state of knowledge by thinking again about that which we initially knew. As he puts it in "Does Moral Philosophy Rest on a Mistake?,"

In order to doubt whether our previous condition was one of knowledge, we have to think of it not as knowledge but as only belief, and our question can only be "Was this belief true?" But as soon as we see that we are thinking of our previous condition as only one of belief, we see that what we are now doubting is not what we first *said* we were doubting, viz., whether a previous condition of knowledge was really knowledge. Hence, to remove the doubt, it is only necessary to appreciate the real nature of our consciousness in apprehending, e.g. that 7 times 4 equals 28, and thereby see that it was no mere condition of believing but a condition of knowing, and then to notice that in our subsequent doubt what we are really doubting is not whether this consciousness was really knowledge, but whether a consciousness of another kind, viz. a belief that 7 times 4 equals 28, was true. (*Moral Writings*, 15)

Thus Prichard's approach to general and moral epistemology really is importantly different from Sidgwick's: Sidgwick is a fallibilist; Prichard is a dogmatist.

Prichard's dogmatism is not the product of adopting a knowledge-first approach in epistemology. It is the product instead of adopting a distinctive version of knowledge-first epistemology. As Timothy Williamson remarks

H.A. Prichard, who also took knowing to be a mental state, held that one is always in a position to know whether one knows or merely believes. . . . Few would now claim such powers of discrimination. Indeed, one cause of denials that knowing is a mental state may be the assumption that one must always be in a position to know whether one is in a given mental state.[20]

The question then is how far Ross inherits Prichard's dogmatism. There are certainly reasons to expect that he might inherit it. After all, he observes in the preface to *The Right and the Good* that

My main obligation is to Professor H.A. Prichard. I believe I owe the main lines of the view expressed in my first two chapters to his article "Does Moral Philosophy Rest on a Mistake?" (RG v)

THE METAETHICAL FRAMEWORK | 183

And the most striking epistemological passages in *The Right and the Good* are to be found in chapter 2.

The obvious place to find dogmatism in Ross (other than in the articulations of the distinctive knowledge-first position he shares with Prichard) is in his views about the status of principles of prima facie duty: his insistence that these (unlike judgments of duty proper) are properly objects of knowledge; that they meet his (and Prichard's) standards of certainty. Whether or not this is the reason or part of the reason why Ross says principles of prima facie duty are objects of knowledge, I shall now argue that his claims about the special epistemic status of principles of prima facie duty are problematic.

7. THE SPECIAL EPISTEMIC STATUS OF PRINCIPLES OF PRIMA FACIE DUTY

As we saw, Ross commits himself to (what I labeled) an "epistemic asymmetry" between our knowledge of the principles of prima facie duty, and our knowledge of duty proper. One of Ross's formulations of an epistemic asymmetry claim is

> Our judgments about our actual duty in concrete situations have none of the certainty that attaches to our recognition of the general principles of duty. (RG 30)

Here the contrast is between our knowledge of prima facie duty and our knowledge of duty proper. In other places, Ross articulates a distinct but related epistemic asymmetry claim, contrasting our knowledge of principles of prima facie duty with our lack of knowledge of the degree of obligatoriness or the relative degree of obligatoriness of different obligations. He says in *The Right and the Good*,

> Where a possible act is seen to have two characteristics, in virtue of one of which it is *prima facie* right, and in virtue of the other *prima facie* wrong, we are (I think) well aware that we are not certain whether we ought or ought not to do it; that whether we do it or not, we are taking a moral risk. (30)

And in the *Foundations*, he says,

> While we *know* certain types of act to be *prima facie* obligatory, we have only opinion about the degree of their obligatoriness. (188)

I shall suggest that while Ross gives an attractive picture of the nature of the key components of judgments of duty, some of his claims about the special epistemic status of principles of prima facie duty are indefensibly strong.

His picture of judgments of duty is that they involve three importantly different kinds of input: empirical information, principles of prima facie duty, and balancing judgments. The empirical information is about the various base characteristics of possible acts. Some of these base characteristics have normative significance. We recognize that they do by grasping principles of prima facie duty. Ross has a distinctive account of the way in which we recognize the normative significance of base characteristics. We usually don't do so by relying explicitly on a general principle. Instead, we directly see the prima facie rightness of an individual act. As he puts it,

> When I reflect on my own attitude towards particular acts,
> I seem to find that it is not by deduction but by direct insight
> that I see them to be right, or wrong. I never seem to be in the
> position of not seeing directly the rightness of a particular act
> of kindness, for instance, and of having to read this off from a
> general principle. (F 171)

Having recognized the morally significant features of different options, we then need to balance or weigh them against one another, to determine which is the more obligatory.

This picture of the nature of moral judgment seems to me attractive. But there are good reasons to doubt some of Ross's strong claims about the special epistemic status of one of its components, judgments of prima facie duty. To see this, consider first the claim that the principles of prima facie duty are special in being the objects of knowledge (as Prichard and Ross conceive knowledge):

> It is proper to use the word 'apprehension' in the . . . case [of
> judgments of the prima facie rightness of certain types of act]. . . .
> That an act, *qua* fulfilling a promise, or *qua* effecting a just distribution of good, or *qua* returning services rendered, or *qua*
> promoting the good of others, or *qua* promoting the virtue or
> insight of the agent, is *prima facie* right is self-evident. (RG 29)

I think that Ross is here mistaken. These principles of prima facie duty do not meet his and Prichard's demanding standards for knowledge according to which knowledge requires complete certainty. To see why, we need to recall what is involved in a principle being a principle of prima facie duty. A principle of prima facie duty does not just say that a certain base property is *correlated* with rightness in the sense that, other things equal, actions with that property tend to be right. It says rather that it is *that base property* that is *right-making.* Consider again Ross's favorite example of a nonconsequentialist principle of prima facie duty. As he expresses it in the preceding quotation, the principle is that "an act, *qua* fulfilling a promise . . . is *prima facie* right." To be certain of this principle, we would need to be certain that no alternative to Ross's view about promising was correct. We would have to be certain that no consequentialist account of the moral importance of promises is correct; we would have to be certain too that no monistic deontological theory that derived the wrongness of breaking promises from some more general deontological principle was correct. I argued briefly earlier in favor of Ross's position, at least as compared to the consequentialist alternative. But I do not think that either Ross or I could claim certainty here. And the same goes for the other special obligations on which (as we have seen) Ross places so much emphasis.

Someone might reply that even if Ross is wrong in claiming certainty for the principles of prima facie duty involving special obligations, we can be certain of the principle of prima facie duty that articulates the general obligation to promote the good. Such a view would not be particularly congenial to Ross himself: though, as I have emphasized, he is not hostile to consequentialism, he would be unlikely to welcome the idea that consequentialist principles of prima facie duty are the objects of knowledge and nonconsequentialist principles of prima facie duty objects of mere right opinion. But here too, I think, no such certainty is available. For while Ross and consequentialists agree that there is a general obligation to promote the good, others do not. Philosophers like Philippa Foot have suggested that all there is instead is a specific and constrained virtue of benevolence.[21] Ross would disagree. I would think he would be right to disagree. But, again, I don't think I could reasonably claim to be certain. That promoting the good is correlated with reasons; that there is at least a secondary principle of promoting the good, need not be in dispute. But it is something more to claim that it is qua promoting the good that actions that do so tend to be right, that it is the property of promoting the good that is itself reason-giving; and this additional thing is not something that we can claim to know, at least according to Ross's standard on which knowledge requires certainty.

So, I suggest, Ross is wrong in claiming that principles of prima facie duty are the objects of knowledge (as he conceives knowledge). But even if principles of prima facie duty are not certain and hence not knowledge by Ross's standards, Ross could still be right in his *comparative* claims: he could still be right that judgments of prima facie duty are *more certain* than balancing judgments, or that they are *more certain* than judgments about our actual duty in concrete situations.

Consider first the comparative claim that judgments of prima facie duty are more certain than balancing judgments. This claim seems to me plausible if construed moderately: that in general judgments of prima facie duty are more certain than balancing judgments. But it is not plausible that *all* judgments of prima facie duty are more certain than *any* balancing judgment. Some balancing judgments involve balancing a trivial consideration against an important consideration. These judgments seem just as certain as paradigm judgments of prima facie duty. While Ross doesn't notice this point in *The Right and the Good*, he does at one place in the *Foundations*:

> In comparing goods, and in comparing *prima facie* duties, while we are often in doubt which is the greater good or the more

> stringent obligation, in other cases, where the one good is *much*
> the greater or the one obligation *much* the more stringent, we
> seem to be able to grasp these facts with certainty. (190–91)

Consider second the comparative claim that judgments
of prima facie duty are more certain than judgments of our
actual duty in concrete situations. This comparative claim
is less problematic than the comparative claim about balancing judgments. For to judge our actual duty in concrete
situations, we don't only need to make balancing judgments.
We also need empirical information. In order to know that
one of two options is correct, we need to know how much
good will be produced by each. That knowledge is difficult
or impossible to acquire, for it is always possible that in the
further future one option will have much better results than
the other in ways that we now cannot foresee.

We should note, though, that this argument applies
only to *judgments of our actual duty in concrete situations*.
In one important way it does not extend to all *judgments
of duty proper*. For at least one familiar kind of judgment
of duty proper in moral philosophy is a judgment about a
fully specified hypothetical case: a case where we get to
specify that there are only (say) three competing claims,
that neither option produces more good than the other in
the further future, etc. Judgments involving such familiar
thought-experiments or hypothetical cases are judgments
of duty proper. But since we can stipulate that in important
ways other things are equal in these hypothetical cases, the
best arguments for Ross's claim that judgments of prima facie
duty are always more certain than judgments of our actual
duty in concrete situations do not extend to such judgments
about fully specified hypothetical cases.

8. DETERMINACY, EPISTEMIC AND METAPHYSICAL

I just argued that in one way Ross is too skeptical about judgments as to the relative weight of different competing prima facie duties. In some cases we can be very confident in these judgments, much more confident than Ross typically allows. I now want to argue that he is in another way not skeptical enough about them. He thinks that problems that arise in weighing competing prima facie duties in difficult cases are purely epistemic. I shall argue instead that the problems are metaphysical.

In Lecture VIII of the *Foundations* Ross defends his view about the level of precision that attaches to judgments about reasons. As I want to put it, his view is that we can (only) make imprecise cardinal judgments. In this part of his discussion Ross begins with issues involving estimating the relative goodness of different pleasures. Here, despite the difficulties represented by disparate pleasures (like the pleasures of pushpin and poetry, to use Bentham's famous example), Ross seems to argue that there is a fully determinate answer, though we can only approximate to grasping it:

> In principle it seem to me that all pleasures fall on one scale in respect of intensity and are comparable in respect of it, though when the pleasures are very different in character it is only a very considerable difference in intensity that one can detect. (F 179–80)

Ross then turns to the relative weight of different *kinds* of goods. He argues against two views which very sharply limit the proper comparisons that can be made. One such view (articulated by H. H. Price) is that the scale for different goods is merely ordinal—we can know what the order is, but not what the relative sizes of any differences are. Ross argues against the view that the scale for goods is merely ordinal by appeal to cases in which we *can* properly compare different options:

> Suppose that only *good* effects are anticipated, and that only three goods are involved, whose order on the scale of goods is A, B, C (A being the nearest to zero), and that we have to choose between two actions, one of which will produce one, and the other two, of these goods. Then if (as the theory in question supposes) we knew only the order, but had no notion of the amount of goodness in any of the three goods, we should know that it was preferable to produce A + C rather than B, and B + C rather than A, but we should have no notion whether it was better to produce A + B rather than C. . . . Now, in practice we are not conscious of this limitation. It certainly sometimes happens that when we think one action will produce a single good and the other a combination of lesser goods we judge without hesitation. (F 181–82)

A second view holds that we know the size of the intervals, so cardinal comparisons are possible, but that there is no meaningful way of assigning a zero point. Ross argues that this again is incompatible with judgments we make. He argues instead that we can make imprecise cardinal comparisons:

> There is, of course, no natural unit of good. But we can arbitrarily take some small good and say that the goods we are comparing are twice, five times, &c., as good as it. Or, without

having any particular unit of good in mind, we can say "whatever unit of good be taken, B would be worth twice as many of it as A, C five times as many as A," and so on.

Now in fact we can never speak with as great precision as that. The position rather is this: the most we can say with confidence is that B is worth not less than m times and not more than n times as much as A, and so on. It is clear that if we have this type of knowledge, then we shall sometimes be able and sometimes be unable to say of good C (for instance) that it is worth more (or less) than A + B. (F 183)

I think Ross is right in these arguments. But he then goes much too far: he claims that the imprecision here is all epistemic rather than metaphysical:

> We should be justified, I think, in supposing that any good contains a definite amount of goodness, but since we cannot estimate this exactly but only as falling within certain limits, our knowledge is often not enough to enable us to compare one greater with two or more lesser goods. And, of course, the same difficulty often makes it impossible to say whether, of two single goods A and B, A or B is greater or A and B are equal. (F 183)

I shall argue that Ross is here mistaken: the imprecision is metaphysical, not epistemic. It is not that there is a precise truth about the goodness of different options which we cannot discover; rather, the only truths available in this area are imprecise. To make this argument, we can draw on some examples and claims of Parfit's. He writes,

> Some reasons are *precisely* comparable in the sense that there are precise truths about their relative weight or strength. . . .

> But when we compare most reasons . . . these reasons are much
> less comparable. (OWM 1, 131–32)

Parfit gives several examples. Of two pains, one short but
much more intense, one much longer but less intense, he
suggests that

> One of these pains could not, for example, be 2.36 times worse
> than the other. Even in principle, there is no scale on which we
> could precisely compare the strengths of our reasons to avoid
> two such different pains. (OWM 1, 132)

Parfit also gives examples involving reasons of more diverse
kinds: economic versus aesthetic reasons, or (more immediately germane to Ross) reasons to keep our promises and to
help strangers.

Parfit's position on such conflicts seems to me much
more plausible than Ross's. Parfit thinks that (a) there are
clear cases, where a trivial reason of one kind competes
against an important reason of another kind. In those cases,
we can be confident in judging the important reason to outweigh the trivial reason, but that (b) there is another range of
cases where there is, even in principle, no right answer as to
the relative weights of reasons of these different kinds. These
two claims seem to me plausible, individually and jointly.
Ross, by contrast, (a) (often though not always) suggests that
epistemically there are no clear cases: every weighing judgment is something like a lucky guess, but (b) claims that metaphysically there is always a fully determinate truth about
the relative weight or strength of reasons of different kinds.
These two claims seem to me implausible individually, and
still more implausible together.

9. CONCLUSION: ROSS'S METAETHICS AND MORAL EPISTEMOLOGY

Ross's metaethics is more satisfactory than his moral episte-mology. His metaethical position is broadly similar to that of predecessors in the nonnaturalist tradition, especially Moore and Sidgwick. But it has distinctive advantages: the emphasis on the distinction between essence theories and grounds theories that is the metaethical corollary of the introduction of the concept of prima facie duty is illuminating; and Ross does well to take on not just the familiar naturalistic essence theories criticized by his predecessors, but also the emerging naturalistic alternatives of noncognitivism and error theory.

His most important distinctive views and claims in moral epistemology are less satisfactory. He inherits from Prichard a version of knowledge-first epistemology that leads to dogmatism. And, whether or not such dogmatism is part of their underlying motivation, Ross's claims about the special epistemic status of judgment of prima facie duty are problematic.

NOTES

1. A. J. Ayer, *Language, Truth, and Logic* (London: Gollancz, 1936), chapter 6; Rudolf Carnap, *Philosophy and Logical Syntax* (London: Kegan Paul, Trench, Trubner, 1935).
2. For Cook Wilson, see John Cook Wilson, *Statement and Inference*, 2 vols. (Oxford: Clarendon Press, 1926). For Prichard see H. A. Prichard, *Knowledge and Perception* (Oxford: Clarendon Press, 1950); Page references will be place in the text. And see also Prichard, *Moral Writings*.
3. At the end of section 14.

4. William Frankena, "The Naturalistic Fallacy," *Mind* 48 (1939): 464–77.
5. On this matter, see the editor's introduction and the preface to the second edition in G. E. Moore, *Principia Ethica*, rev ed., ed. Thomas Baldwin (Cambridge: Cambridge University Press, 1993). Page references will be placed in the text.
6. See, most famously, "Internal and External Reasons," in Bernard Williams, *Moral Luck* (Cambridge: Cambridge University Press, 1981), 101–13.
7. Particularly G. E Moore, *Ethics* (Oxford: Oxford University Press, 1912) and G. E. Moore, "The Conception of Intrinsic Value," in G. E. Moore, *Philosophical Studies* (London: Routledge and Kegan Paul, 1922).
8. Broad remarks in "A Reply to My Critics" (*Broad's Critical Essays in Moral Philosophy*, 307): "As a student at Cambridge I was brought up to believe that it is a fundamentally important proposition of ethics that moral attributes belong to a peculiar category called 'non-natural', and that there is something called 'the naturalistic fallacy', which most moralists had committed before the light dawned in 1903. When I became Professor of Moral Philosophy, and had to write a course of lectures on ethics, I was unable to discover any intelligible and tenable account of the meaning of this distinction between 'natural' and 'non-natural' attributes. It also seemed to me that, unless 'fallacy' be used in the improper and question-begging sense of 'mistaken opinion', instead of in its proper sense of 'invalid bit of reasoning', there was nothing which can be described as 'the naturalistic fallacy'."
9. Classic presentations of the Cornell realist view are Richard Boyd, "How to Be a Moral Realist" in Geoffrey Sayre-McCord, ed., *Essays on Moral Realism* (Ithaca, NY: Cornell University Press, 1988), 181–228; David Brink, *Moral Realism and the Foundations of Ethics* (Cambridge: Cambridge University Press, 1989); Nicholas Sturgeon, "Moral Explanations," in Sayre-McCord, *Essays on Moral Realism*, 229–55. Schroeder develops his view in *Slaves of the Passions* (Oxford: Oxford University Press, 2007).
10. For Nagel, see particularly *The View from Nowhere*, chapter 8. For Parfit, see Normativity," *Oxford Studies in Metaethics* 1

(2006): 325–80 and OWM 2, part 6; the more metaethically ecumenical Parfit of *On What Matters*, vol. 3 (Oxford: Oxford University Press, 2017) has less in common with Ross. For Scanlon see *Being Realistic about Reasons* (Oxford: Oxford University Press, 2014).

11. On this point, see Hurka, *British Ethical Theorists*, 104–5. For Geach see P. T. Geach, "Ascriptivism," *Philosophical Review* 69 (1960): 221–25; P. T. Geach, "Assertion," *Philosophical Review* 74 (1965): 449–65; P. T. Geach, "Imperative and Deontic Logic," *Analysis* 18 (1958): 49–56. Ross's formulation of the problem is often not noted at all, as for instance in Mark Schroeder's excellent overview "What Is the Frege-Geach Problem," *Philosophy Compass* 3–4 (2008): 703–20.

12. The most celebrated articulation of error theory is of course in chapter 1 of John Mackie, *Ethics* (Harmondsworth: Penguin, 1977). But Mackie originally (and much less famously) advanced the view in "A Refutation of Morals," *Australasian Journal of Philosophy* 24 (1946): 77–90. He remarks on page 20 of *Ethics* in the section headed "Is Objectivity a Real Issue?" that the issue "was discussed vigorously in the nineteen thirties and forties, but since then has received much less attention." Ross can be seen as contributing to that discussion.

13. See Sharon Street, "A Darwinian Dilemma for Realist Theories of Value," *Philosophical Studies* 127.1 (2006): 109–66. For one response, see Parfit, OWM 2, chapter 33.

14. I will use the terms "fallibilist" and "dogmatist" in this section as Hurka does. To be a fallibilist in this sense is to think that apparently self-evident intuitions can be mistaken. To be a dogmatist in this sense is to think that intuitions cannot be mistaken. The terms are used rather differently in contemporary epistemology. Fallibilism there is the view that knowledge does not require conclusive reasons, certainty, or ruling out of the possibility of error; dogmatism is the view that simply having certain experiences is enough to give you prima facie justification. Important work includes Stewart Cohen, "How to Be a Fallibilist," *Philosophical Perspectives* 2 (1988): 91–123; James Pryor, "The Skeptic and the Dogmatist," *Noûs* 34 (2000): 517–49.

15. On this, see my *Sidgwickian Ethics* (New York: Oxford University Press, 2011), chapter 4.
16. Henry Sidgwick, "Verification of Beliefs," in Henry Sidgwick, *Essays on Ethics and Method*, ed. Marcus G. Singer (Oxford: Oxford University Press, 2000), 121.
17. Sidgwick, "Verification of Beliefs," 121.
18. Henry Sidgwick, "Further on the Criteria of Truth and Error," in *Essays on Ethics and Method*, 166.
19. Henry Sidgwick, "The Establishment of Ethical First Principles," in *Essays on Ethics and Method*, 32.
20. Timothy Williamson, *Knowledge and Its Limits* (Oxford: Oxford University Press, 2000), 23.
21. Philippa Foot, "Utilitarianism and the Virtues," in Samuel Scheffler, ed., *Consequentialism and Its Critics* (Oxford: Oxford University Press, 1988), 224–42.

BIBLIOGRAPHY

Anscombe, G. E. M. "Modern Moral Philosophy." *Philosophy* 33 (1958): 1–19.

Audi, Robert. *The Good in the Right*. Princeton: Princeton University Press, 2004.

Ayer, A. J. *Language, Truth, and Logic*. London: Gollancz, 1936.

Bakhurst, David, Hooker, Brad, and Little, Margaret Olivia, eds. *Thinking about Reasons: Themes from the Philosophy of Jonathan Dancy*. Oxford: Oxford University Press, 2013.

Boyd, Richard. "How to Be a Moral Realist." In Sayre-McCord, *Essays on Moral Realism*, 181–228.

Bradford, Gwen. *Achievement*. Oxford: Oxford University Press, 2015.

Broad, C. D. *Broad's Critical Essays in Moral Philosophy*. Edited by David R. Cheney. London: George Allen & Unwin, 1971.

Broad, C. D. "Critical Notice of W. D. Ross, *Foundations of Ethics*." *Mind* 49 (1940): 228–39.

Broad, C. D. *Ethics*. Edited by C. Lewy. Dordrecht: Martinus Nijhoff, 1985.

Broad, C. D. *Five Types of Ethical Theory*. London: Kegan Paul, 1930.

Brown, Campbell. "Consequentialize This!" *Ethics* 121.4 (2011): 739–71.

Butler, Joseph. *Fifteen Sermons & Other Writings on Ethics*. Edited by David McNaughton. Oxford: Oxford University Press, 2017.

Carnap, Rudolf. *Philosophy and Logical Syntax*. London: Kegan, Paul, Trench, Trubner, 1935.

Cohen, Stewart. "How to Be a Fallibilist." *Philosophical Perspectives* 2 (1988): 91–123.

Cook Wilson, John. *Statement and Inference*. 2 vols. Oxford: Clarendon Press, 1926.

Crisp, Roger. "The Dualism of Practical Reason." *Proceedings of the Aristotelian Society* 96 (1996): 53–73.

Crisp, Roger. *Reasons and the Good*. Oxford: Clarendon Press, 2006.

Dancy, Jonathan. *Ethics without Principles*. Oxford: Clarendon Press, 2004.

Dancy, Jonathan. *Moral Reasons*. Oxford: Blackwell, 1993.

Dancy, Jonathan. "More Right than Wrong." In Timmons and Johnson, *Reason, Value, and Respect*, 101–18.

Darwall, Stephen. *Morality, Authority, and Law: Essays in Second Personal Ethics*. Vol. 1. Oxford: Oxford University Press, 2013.

Darwall, Stephen. "Morality's Distinctiveness." In Darwall, *Morality, Authority, and Law*, 3–19.

Dreier, James, ed. *Blackwell Contemporary Debates in Moral Theory*. Oxford: Blackwell, 2006.

Dreier, James. "In Defense of Consequentializing." In Mark Timmons, ed., *Oxford Studies in Normative Ethics*, vol. 1. New York: Oxford University Press, 2011: 97–119.

Ewing, A. C. *Second Thoughts in Moral Philosophy*. London: Routledge and Kegan Paul, 1959.

Foot, Philippa. "Utilitarianism and the Virtues." In Scheffler, *Consequentialism and Its Critics*, 224–42.

Frankena, William. "The Naturalistic Fallacy." *Mind* 48 (1939): 464–77.

Geach, P. T. "Ascriptivism." *Philosophical Review* 69 (1960): 221–25.

Geach, P. T. "Assertion." *Philosophical Review* 74 (1965): 449–65.

Geach, P. T. "Imperative and Deontic Logic." *Analysis* 18 (1958): 49–56.

Gert, Joshua. "Requiring and Justifying: Two Dimensions of Normative Strength." *Erkenntnis* 59 (2003): 5–36.

Gibbard, Allan. *Wise Choices, Apt Feelings.* Cambridge MA: Harvard University Press, 1990.

Henning, Tim and Paytas, Tyler, eds. *Essays on Kant and Sidgwick.* Routledge, forthcoming.

Hooker, Brad and Little, Margaret Olivia, eds. *Moral Particularism.* Oxford: Clarendon Press, 2000.

Hurka, Thomas. "Audi's Marriage of Ross and Kant." In Timmons, Greco, and Mele, *Rationality and the Good,* 64–72.

Hurka, Thomas. *British Ethical Theorists from Sidgwick to Ewing.* Oxford: Oxford University Press, 2014.

Hurka, Thomas. "Moore in the Middle." *Ethics* 113.3 (2003): 599–628.

Hurka, Thomas. "Sidgwick on Consequentialism and Deontology." *Utilitas* 26.2 (2014): 129–52.

Hurka, Thomas, ed. *Underivative Duty.* Oxford: Oxford University Press, 2011.

Hurka, Thomas. *Virtue, Vice, and Value.* Oxford: Oxford University Press, 2001.

Kagan, Shelly. *The Limits of Morality.* Oxford: Clarendon Press, 1989.

Kamm, Frances. *Intricate Ethics.* Oxford: Oxford University Press, 2008.

Kant, Immanuel. *Grounding for the Metaphysics of Morals.* Translated by James W. Ellington. Indianapolis: Hackett, 1993.

Kavka, Gregory. *Hobbesian Moral and Political Theory.* Princeton: Princeton University Press, 1986.

Louden, Robert. "Towards a Genealogy of 'Deontology'." *Journal of the History of Philosophy* 34.4 (1996): 571–92.

Mackie, J. L. *Ethics.* Harmondsworth: Penguin, 1977.

Mackie, J. L. "A Refutation of Morals." *Australasian Journal of Philosophy* 24 (1946): 77–90.

McCloskey, H. J. "Ross and the Concept of a *Prima Facie* Duty." *Australasian Journal of Philosophy* 41.3 (1963): 336–45.

McNaughton, D. "An Unconnected Heap of Duties?" In Stratton-Lake, *Ethical Intuitionism,* 76–91.

McNaughton, D. and Rawling, P. "Agent-Relativity and the Doing-Happening Distinction." *Philosophical Studies* 63.2 (1991): 167–85.

McNaughton, D. and Rawling, P. "Contours of the Practical Landscape." In Bakhurst, Hooker, and Little, *Thinking about Reasons*, 240–64.

McNaughton, D. and Rawling, P. "Unprincipled Ethics." In Hooker and Little, *Moral Particularism*, 256–75.

Mill, J. S. *Utilitarianism*. In Troyer, *The Classical Utilitarians*, 95–149.

Moore, G. E. *Ethics*. Oxford: Oxford University Press, 1921.

Moore, G. E. *Philosophical Studies*. London: Routledge and Kegan Paul, 1922.

Moore, G. E. *Principia Ethica*. Cambridge: Cambridge University Press, 1903.

Moore, G. E. *Principia Ethica*. Rev. ed. Cambridge: Cambridge University Press, 1993.

Nagel, Thomas. *The View from Nowhere*. New York: Oxford University Press, 1986.

Norcross, Alastair. "Reasons without Demands: Rethinking Rightness." In Dreier, *Blackwell Contemporary Debates in Moral Theory*, 38–53.

Nozick, Robert. *Anarchy, State, and Utopia*. New York: Basic Books, 1974.

Oliveira, Luis. "Rossian Totalism about Intrinsic Value." *Philosophical Studies* 173 (2016): 2069–86.

Olsen, Kristian. "Ross and the Particularism/Generalism Divide." *Canadian Journal of Philosophy* 44.1 (2014): 56–75.

Parfit, Derek. "Normativity." *Oxford Studies in Metaethics* 1 (2006): 325–80.

Parfit, Derek. *On What Matters*. 2 vols. Oxford: Oxford University Press, 2011.

Parfit, Derek. *On What Matters*. Vol. 3. Oxford: Oxford University Press, 2017.

Phillips, David. "Sidgwick's Kantian Account ofMoral Motivation." Forthcoming in Henning and Paytas, *Essays on Kant and Sidgwick*.

Phillips, David. *Sidgwickian Ethics*. New York: Oxford University Press, 2011.

Pickard-Cambridge, W. A. "Two Problems about Duty (I.)." *Mind* 41.161 (1932): 72–96.

Pickard-Cambridge, W. A. "Two Problems about Duty (II.)." *Mind* 41.162 (1932): 145–72.

Pickard-Cambridge, W. A. "Two Problems about Duty (III.)." *Mind* 41.163 (1932): 311–40.

Portmore, Douglas W. *Commonsense Consequentialism.* New York: Oxford University Press, 2011.

Portmore, Douglas W. "Consequentializing Moral Theories." *Pacific Philosophical Quarterly* 88 (2007): 39–73.

Price, Richard. *A Review of the Principal Questions of Morals.* Edited by D. D. Raphael. Oxford: Clarendon Press, 1974.

Prichard, H. A. "Does Moral Philosophy Rest on a Mistake?" In Prichard, *Moral Writings.*

Prichard, H. A. "Duty and Ignorance of Fact." In Prichard, *Moral Writings*, 84–101.

Prichard, H. A. *Knowledge and Perception.* Oxford: Clarendon Press, 1950.

Prichard, H. A. *Moral Writings.* Edited by Jim MacAdam. Oxford: Clarendon Press, 2002.

Pritchard, Duncan. "Recent Work on Epistemic Value." *American Philosophical Quarterly* 44.2 (2007): 85–110.

Pryor, James. "The Skeptic and the Dogmatist." *Noûs* 34 (2000): 517–49.

Rashdall, Hastings. *The Theory of Good and Evil.* Oxford: Oxford University Press, 1907.

Raz, Joseph, ed. *Practical Reasoning.* Oxford: Oxford University Press, 1978.

Ross, W. D. *Aristotle.* London: Methuen, 1923.

Ross, W. D. "The Basis of Objective Judgments in Ethics." *International Journal of Ethics* 37.2 (1927): 113–27.

Ross, W. D. "The Coherence Theory of Goodness." *Proceedings of the Aristotelian Society: Supplementary Volumes* 10 (1931): 61–70.

Ross, W. D. "The Ethics of Punishment." *Journal of Philosophical Studies* 4.14 (1929): 205–11.

Ross, W. D. *Foundations of Ethics.* Oxford: Clarendon Press, 1939.

Ross, W. D. "Is There a Moral End?" *Proceedings of the Aristotelian Society: Supplementary Volumes* 8 (1928): 91–98.

Ross, W. D. *Kant's Ethical Theory.* Oxford: Clarendon Press, 1954.

Ross, W. D. "The Nature of Morally Good Action." *Proceedings of the Aristotelian Society*. New Series 29 (1928–29): 251–74.

Ross, W. D. *The Right and the Good*. Oxford: Clarendon Press, 1930.

Sayre-McCord, Geoffrey, ed. *Essays on Moral Realism*. Ithaca, NY: Cornell University Press, 1988.

Scanlon, Thomas. *Being Realistic about Reasons*. Oxford: Oxford University Press, 2014.

Scanlon, Thomas. *What We Owe to Each Other*. Cambridge, MA: Harvard University Press, 1998.

Scheffler, Samuel, ed. *Consequentialism and Its Critics*. Oxford: Oxford University Press, 1988.

Scheffler, Samuel. *The Rejection of Consequentialism*. Oxford: Oxford University Press, 1982.

Schroeder, Mark. *Slaves of the Passions*. Oxford: Oxford University Press, 2007.

Schroeder, Mark. "Teleology, Agent-Relative Value, and 'Good.'" *Ethics* 117 (2007): 265–95.

Schroeder, Mark. "What Is the Frege-Geach Problem." *Philosophy Compass* 3–4 (2008): 703–20.

Schultz, Bart. "Review of Thomas Hurka, ed. *Underivative Duty*." *British Journal for the History of Philosophy* 20.6 (2012): 1223–26.

Searle, John. "How to Derive 'Ought' from 'Is.'" *Philosophical Review* 73 (1964): 43–58.

Searle, John. "*Prima Facie* Obligations." In Raz, *Practical Reasoning*, 81–90.

Selby-Bigge, L. A. *British Moralists*. 2 vols. Oxford: Clarendon Press, 1897.

Shaver, Robert. "Ross on Self and Others." *Utilitas* 26.3 (2014): 303–20.

Shaver, Robert. "Sidgwick's Axioms and Consequentialism." *Philosophical Review* 123.2 (2014): 173–04.

Sidgwick, Henry. *Essays on Ethics and Method*. Edited by Marcus G. Singer. Oxford: Oxford University Press, 2000.

Sidgwick, Henry. *The Methods of Ethics*. 7th ed. London: Macmillan, 1907.

Singer, Peter. *Practical Ethics*. 3rd ed. Cambridge: Cambridge University Press, 2011.

Skelton, Anthony. "W. D. Ross." *Stanford Encyclopedia of Philosophy*. Summer 2012 ed.

Smith, Michael. *The Moral Problem*. Oxford: Blackwell, 1994.

Steinbock, Bonnie and Norcross, Alastair, eds. *Killing and Letting Die*. New York: Fordham University Press, 1994.

Stratton-Lake, Philip, ed. *Ethical Intuitionism*. Oxford: Clarendon Press, 2002.

Stratton-Lake, Philip. "Pleasure and Reflection in Ross's Intuitionism." In Stratton-Lake, *Ethical Intuitionism*, 113–36.

Strawson, P. F. *The Bounds of Sense*. London: Methuen, 1966.

Street, Sharon. "A Darwinian Dilemma for Realist Theories of Value." *Philosophical Studies* 127.1 (2006): 109–66.

Sturgeon, Nicholas. "Moral Explanations." In Sayre-McCord, *Essays on Moral Realism*, 229–55.

Timmerman, Jens. "What's Wrong with 'Deontology'?" *Proceedings of the Aristotelian Society* 115 (2015): 75–92.

Timmons, Mark, Greco, John, and Mele, Al, eds. *Rationality and the Good*. Oxford: Oxford University Press, 2007.

Timmons, Mark, and Johnson, Robert N., eds. *Reason, Value, and Respect*. Oxford: Oxford University Press, 2015.

Troyer, John, ed. *The Classical Utilitarians*. Indianapolis, IN: Hackett, 2003.

Urmson, J. O. "A Defense of Intuitionism." *Proceedings of the Aristotelian Society* 75 (1975): 111–19.

Williams, Bernard. "Internal and External Reasons." In Williams, *Moral Luck*, 101–13.

Williams, Bernard. *Moral Luck*. Cambridge: Cambridge University Press, 1981.

Williams, Bernard. "Persons, Character, and Morality." In Williams, *Moral Luck*, 1–19.

Williamson, Timothy. *Knowledge and Its Limits*. Oxford: Oxford University Press, 2000.

INDEX

dogmatic intuitionism and, 15,
91–92, 178–79
Prichard and, 156–57, 177–78,
182, 183
Ross and, 177–78, 182, 183, 193
dualism of practical reason
(Sidgwick), 33
dual-source view (Crisp), 75
"Duty and Ignorance of Fact"
(Prichard), 45, 46, 47
duty proper
conceptual fundamentality
and, 42
degree of obligatoriness
and, 24–25
epistemic fundamentality
and, 42–43
force metaphor and, 24–25
knowledge and, 156–57, 183–84
metaphysical fundamentality
and, 42
morally significant properties
of alternative possible acts
and, 22
moral obligation and, 33–34
practical fundamentality
and, 43–44
prima facie duty and, 13,
17–18, 20–23, 24–26,
41–43, 156–57, 175–77
reason and, 33–34
toti-resultant attributes
and, 25–26

egoism
Broad and, 77–79
incoherence objection
regarding, 77–79
Moore's critique of, 78, 79, 81
rational egoism and, 33
Sidgwick on, 74–75, 91–92
utilitarianism and, 91

error theory, 155–56, 166, 167–68,
169, 193
essence theories
arguments relevant to, 173, 174
attitudinal essence theories
and, 173
grounds theories compared to,
155–56, 157–59, 160–61, 169
Ross's argument against various
forms of, 173
Ross's assimilation of grounds
theories with, 171, 174
subjectivism and, 172–73
Ethics without Principles
(Dancy), 98–100
evolutionary debunking
argument, 168–69
Ewing, A.C., 5, 16, 149
experience machine thought
experiment (Nozick), 147–48

fallibilism (Sidgwick), 177–80, 182
Five Types of Ethical Theory
(Broad), 5, 15–16, 57, 98
Foot, Philippa, 186–87
Foundations of Ethics (Ross)
on activities as an intrinsic
good, 148–50
attitudinal definition of
rightness and, 164–65
attitudinal grounds theories
and, 173–74
on avoidance of pain, 30, 31, 74
on Broad, 5–6, 57–58
consequentialism and, 128–29
on deduction from general
principles, 42–43
on desires, 132–34, 135, 136–37
egoistic hedonism rejected in, 165
error theory and, 167, 193
evolutionary definition of
rightness and, 164

ideal utilitarianism
agent-relative intensifiers and,
6–8, 66–67
character of duty and, 6–8
classical deontology and, 96
consequentialism and, 58–59
grounds theories and, 170–71
intrinsic goods and, 2
monistic utilitarianism
contrasted with, 107–8
Ross's critique of, 58–59, 64,
66–67, 85, 87, 90, 96, 170–71

Kagan, Shelley
agent-centered options and, 92
on deontological constraints, 80,
81, 82–84, 92
duty of non-malfeasance and, 88
extremist (straightforwardly
consequentialism) morality
and, 80, 92
ordinary (moderate) morality
critiqued by, 80–81, 82, 86,
87–88, 92
pro tanto reason to promote the
good and, 80–81, 92
Kant, Immanuel
categorical imperative and, 95
consequentialism and, 1–2,
8–9, 95, 98
on motives, 131–32, 134–35
Ross and, 98, 131–32, 134–35
value-based intuitionism and, 4,
94–95, 97
virtue and, 115–16
Kavka, Gregory, 3–4
knowledge
duty proper and,
156–57, 183–84
factual knowledge and, 142,
143, 146
insight and, 142, 145–46

knowledge-first epistemology
and, 142, 145, 183, 193
moderate pluralism about the
good and, 115, 116,
118–19, 127, 128–29,
141–46, 148, 149–50
prima facie duty and, 156–57,
183–84, 185, 187
right opinion and, 142,
143–45, 146
value problem and, 143

limited pluralism about the good.
See moderate pluralism about
the good
limited pluralism about the right.
See moderate pluralism about
the right
The Limits of Morality (Kagan), 80,
82, 87–88

Mackie, John, 27, 167
McCloskey, H. J., 18, 19
McNaughton, David
benefits and, 106
categorization of reasons by,
101, 105–6
classical deontology and,
61, 105–6
default reason and, 100–1, 102
invariant reasons and, 100–3
nonmoral definition of promises
and, 104–5
particularism critiqued
by, 99–100
on promise-keeping, 105
right-tending and wrong-
tending characteristics
for, 103
on weak moral principles, 100
weighting of reasons proposed
by, 101